Other Books by Erika V. Shearin Karres, Ed.D.

Violence Proof Your Kids Now
Make Your Kids Smarter

A⁺TEACHERS

*How to Empower
Your Child's Teacher
and Your Child
to Excel*

Erika V. Shearin Karres, Ed.D.

**Andrews McMeel
Publishing**

Kansas City

Book design by Pete Lippincott

03 04 05 06 07 VAI 10 9 8 7 6 5 4 3 2 1

Library of Congress Cataloging-in-Publication Data

Karres, Erika V. Shearin.
    A+ teachers : does your child's teacher make the grade? : how to
  empower your child's teacher, and your child, to excellence / Erika V.
  Shearin Karres.
        p. cm.
    Includes bibliographical references.
    ISBN 0-7407-3523-3
     1. Teachers—Rating of. 2. Education —Parent participation. I. Title.

  LB2838.K36 2003
  371.14'4—dc21

                                                            2003042136

ATTENTION: SCHOOLS AND BUSINESSES

Andrews McMeel books are available at quantity discounts with bulk purchase for educational, business, or sales promotional use. For information, please write to: Special Sales Department, Andrews McMeel Publishing, 4520 Main Street, Kansas City, Missouri 64111.

Teachers affect eternity.
They can never tell where their influence stops.

—HENRY ADAMS, *THE EDUCATION OF HENRY ADAMS*

The educated differ from the uneducated as much as
the living differ from the dead.

—ARISTOTLE

Those having torches will pass them on to others.

—PLATO, *THE REPUBLIC*

Teaching means helping the child reach his [or her] potential.

—ERICH FROMM

This book is for the millions of parents and teachers who work so hard every day to ensure that all children reach their potential.

And for my daughters,
Elizabeth Shearin Hounshell and Dr. Mary D. Shearin,
and my husband, Andrew Matthew Karres.

Contents

Prologue

Tell me, I forget.
Show me, I remember.
Involve me, I understand.
                    —CHINESE PROVERB

WELCOME TO THE WINNERS' CIRCLE. You belong in it. That's for sure because you're a winner: that is, a person who is successful. And successful you definitely are.

How do I know? I know because you picked up this book, which is a first: an eye-opening look at the secret world of teachers. It takes a winner to step up and tackle the kind of cutting-edge topic that deals with this question: *Does Your Child's Teacher Make the Grade?* But be warned. You will become involved.

It's worrisome to think there might be some teachers working right now in the nation's schools who perhaps don't make the grade. Who are not as good as they should be. We'd all like to think that each and every teacher is fully qualified. But the truth is, we really don't know. Sure, we've all read reports that maybe some teachers don't measure up. We've even heard horror stories of poorly qualified school staffers. But what clear evidence do we have as individual parents? None.

Until now, that is. By the end of this book you'll know what it takes to be a good teacher. You will be well versed in the key teaching strengths, and you'll be able to tell very quickly what makes teachers great. With that knowledge in hand, you'll see which teachers pass with flying colors and which need help. And then you can do just that: help teachers do their job and improve the state of education today. This is where your involvement comes in. I did warn you, didn't I?

Back to that winners' circle. You're a member of it no matter who you are—parent, teacher, grandparent, or concerned community member. That includes everyone interested in kids, and everyone interested in the future of our country.

Why?

Because this book is all about our children and how well prepared they will be to shape the future and the world. With so much at stake, it's of the utmost importance that we examine their daily lives, the greater part of which is spent in school with school personnel. Indeed, from age three or four on, most children spend the majority of their waking hours in the company of teachers. So doesn't it make sense to know as much as possible about them?

What do teachers do all day long? What really makes them tick?

Let's find out!

Not long ago, the world of medicine was a closed chapter for most people. They went to the doctor, sure, but they were in awe of health professionals. Indeed, many patients back then were afraid to ask their physicians why they did what they did or how they determined their diagnoses.

Fortunately, over the last few decades, a change occurred. These days many people march into their doctor's office, a long list of questions in hand. Whole books have been published on taking charge of one's health. What a world of difference that has made! Patients today are much more knowledgeable about their well-being. And when they move, they often know exactly what kind of general practitioner they're looking for.

The same isn't true of schools.

Why not? One reason is that most parents don't have a choice about where to send their kids. They live in a specific school district, and that automatically dictates the school their kids will attend. In effect, many parents feel they're victims of the educational system. All they can do is grin—or grimace—and bear it.

But no more. From this moment on, parents will have the upper hand. They will be victorious. They can take charge of the education their kids receive. First they will inform themselves; then they will empower themselves, and as a result they will effect change. Yes! For the first time a book can show them how, step by simple step. And *A + Teachers* is the book.

So thanks for picking it up, and also congratulations to you! You're moving forward in a big way, for yourself and for others. In thirty minutes or so, you'll know exactly how to get started in obtaining the best education possible for your child; by the end of this book you'll be truly powerful and able to work for educational excellence, not only for your child but for all kids in your neighborhood, your town, your state, your country. You will succeed. You're already succeeding. With every page you read, you're forging ahead.

One part of being a winner is having courage, and you do. You're not afraid of a challenge, even though the process may include pushing the envelope or taking a little time out of your busy schedule. You already know that nothing worthwhile can be accomplished without effort. And you're willing to give a few extra minutes to improve what's most important today—education. You step up gladly to meet this brand-new exciting challenge: to do for education what's been done for medicine.

We're going to go behind the scenes and find out what's really going on in the classroom, the teachers' lounge, and the office, not just during the annual open house but every day of the school year. More than likely, all will be well. Your child's teacher or teachers will turn out to be tops. Your child's school will run like a well-oiled piece of first-rate machinery. But if that's not the case, you can get busy and make a major contribution. After all, you're a winner. That means you have extra-special qualities. Let's put them to use.

To start, ask yourself: Am I happy with the state of our schools? Are my kids making the honor roll or at least consistently aiming for it? Are they realizing their true potential? Or—as in so many families these days—are they smart yet bringing home only so-so grades? If that's the case, stop worrying right now, because you're going to get involved.

Let's face it: While most everything else in this country during the past few decades has advanced—been upgraded, updated, moved ahead, or led forward—many of our schools have stood still since the sixties. That has caused our nation's youth to emerge from high school undereducated, undermotivated, and unprepared to face the future.

You will now do your share to stop this trend. You will educate yourself and ensure that the education your kids get will be mediocre no more. It's easy, really. All you have to do is familiarize yourself with the five basic teaching skills—I call them strengths—every teacher needs to master. Then see how your kids' teachers measure up. And then—through your work with teachers, the school administration and other staff, and the PTA, and via your voice with the school board—support great teaching wholeheartedly. Insist that all teachers in your kids' school get those teaching skills right now, if they don't already possess them. And get the community and financial support they need and the respect they deserve.

In short, here in your hand is the only tool you need. By the time you finish this groundbreaking book, you will

- understand for the first time what's really involved in teaching,
- be able to improve your kids' schools,
- know how better to support your kids' teachers and their work,
- raise the level of instruction for all kids,
- become a more education-committed parent, and best of all,
- be able to inspire your own children to surge ahead to do their utmost academically.

Now are you ready? Ready to win?

Personal Note In 1945 in post–World War II Germany, all schools were destroyed. Before his suicide, Adolf Hitler had decreed that all of Germany would become "scorched earth." That's why not only the factories but also the few schools that hadn't been bombed out already were leveled by the Nazis.

But after the war was over, the schools slowly opened up again. Often it was just a building in ruins with the roof patched, the rubble swept aside, and a few wooden planks on cinder blocks for benches.

That was the case in Diessen am Ammersee, a small Bavarian town near the Alps, where the Catholic nuns reopened school. And my! What a motley crew showed up on that first day: starved little urchins, struck silent, with sunken-in eyes and running sores, filthy and wearing rags. Quite a few had a part of an arm or leg missing. There were still many land mines buried along the roads and in the countryside for kids to step on.

But no matter what their looks, the children crammed into the one large room and crowded onto the makeshift benches. Since books and other materials were destroyed, the nuns cut

paper bags into squares and handed them out. Also, a few pencils
had been found, which the school kids were told to share.

An old cracked blackboard had also survived the bombing.
Each day, before school, the nuns copied a paragraph from a
famous writer on this board and listed the author beneath it. One
day it was Goethe, another day Schiller, a third day Shakespeare,
then Mark Twain. Each day, they covered the paragraph with an
old sheet. While the first graders practiced their ABCs, a nun dic-
tated the paragraph for the day to all those kids who could
already read and write. Afterward she yanked off the sheet, reveal-
ing the day's short literary selection, which the kids had tried to
write on their own by listening to the nun. Then came the hard
work: Each child had to write every misspelled word ten times.

I was one of those children. But unlike the rest of the class, I
didn't do any better as the weeks progressed and food became
more plentiful.

The other kids quickly came out of their shock, gained
weight, and started to smile and play. In contrast, I withdrew
more and more into myself. The war had robbed me of my
mother and robbed my father of his sanity. With ten boisterous
brothers and sisters, I never got enough to eat. I had rickets. And
there was no end to the misery in sight. Sure, World War II was
over for the other kids. In my case, it had only changed loca-
tions and now raged in my house. So at age six I became mute,
just a shadow—a little, skinny, scabby girl who hardly ever made
a sound.

Not that anybody noticed. There were too many other live-
lier kids around who got all the attention, at home and in
school. I could have faded away completely and nobody would
have noticed.

That's exactly what I was doing until one special morning.
I'd just crept into the schoolroom when the nun started dictat-
ing the day's paragraph. I wrote it down as best I could, then

glanced up at the board where, after the sheet was removed, it appeared written in the nun's beautiful handwriting.

Then I felt a flash of recognition. Oh! Wasn't that selection on the board strangely familiar? I looked from the board back to my work and back at the board again. Each time I could feel my heart beating a little faster, and then I knew why. There on the board was my name in capital letters! On this day, this wonderful, special day, the nun had chosen part of a story I'd written and turned in for homework. She must have noticed that little silent child in the back of the room after all and been determined to recognize her in some way.

It worked. How it worked! I started feeling hope for the first time, woke from my trauma state, smiled a little, and said something to my classmates. Soon I started demanding my share of food at home. I lifted my face and stared back at the world, ready to tackle what I could.

And all because one teacher had observed the pitiful state I was in and found a way to jolt me out of it.

Needless to say, I became a teacher. After coming to the United States at age twenty-one, I still remembered the warm feeling I had had years ago when Sister Gertrude went out of her way to make me feel special. I wanted to be part of a profession that had so much power and such a lasting influence, so I taught school for thirty years in Orange County, North Carolina. After that I started working in teacher training at the University of North Carolina in Chapel Hill, which I still continue to do.

That's given me thirty-seven wonderful uninterrupted years in teaching—so far. I've been actively involved in education for well over a third of a century as a practicing teacher, and for over fifty-seven years, if we include my years as a student.

You could say I have devoted my whole life to education. My special strength is school improvement: motivating parents, teachers, and students to give their best efforts. Therefore, since the mid-1960s, I've chronicled the classroom practices of outstanding educators and the actions of committed parents and outstanding students. And I have written extensively in columns and books about school success and student smarts.

Some people call me the School Doctor, others just Dr. Erika, but what I am called is unimportant. What matters is that, as the result of a lifetime spent teaching students, teaching teachers and parents, and doing teacher-evaluation research, I have developed a simple five-part teaching skills measurement, which I am pleased to share with you.

Now you see why I wrote this book and why I'm passing on my insider information. I want this scoop to empower *you*, so you can step up and become a hero.

Will you?

User Guide

MANY STATES USE A COMPREHENSIVE teacher observation form that has fifty or more items on it to be checked. That means when an evaluator strides into any classroom in the nation, he or she can record if and when those fifty or more competencies are observed. Then, according to the result, the teacher who's being rated may or may not get a summary statement of his or her skills.

When teachers apply for teaching positions, similar forms are used. These forms, often entitled Confidential Evaluation of Performance, Competence, and Character, are references that teachers must submit from their previous employers. But all they have is tiny spaces for numerous little Xes, and hardly any space for explanations and commentaries. Therefore, teachers—both beginners and real pros—are very often underrated. Furthermore, the rating scale used for teacher assessments is frequently ridiculous.

Here is an example. The person rating a teacher's ability is instructed as follows: *Please check the level at which the applicant consistently performs. Is it:*

☐ unsatisfactory?

☐ below expectations?

☐ at expectations?

☐ above expectations?

☐ superior?

I say, Who is to know?

In other states or counties, the teacher performance rating scales include these rubrics: *Is the teacher's work*

- ☐ unsatisfactory?
- ☐ below standard?
- ☐ at standard?
- ☐ above standard?
- ☐ well above standard?
- ☐ superior?

Again I say, who knows? Naturally, all those teacher forms and assessment instruments serve a purpose, but they don't tell what's really going on in the classroom.

What does *at expectations* or *below standard* really mean? Do you know? I admit I don't, and I've been working with quality teaching for close to forty years. Of course, I have an idea; it's my purpose to clue you in because nowadays you need to know. But, trust me, I'm not going to bore you with lots of out-dated research and the results of studies that never went any-where. You're not going to be exposed to a vague rating scale and never-ending lists of obscure topics in educationese to learn more about what teachers do and how they measure up.

Tell me honestly. Does it help you to know that your child's teacher was rated as *above standard* on logical sequencing, and *at expectations* in the assumption of noninstructional duties or ethics? No way. What you want to know is, How well can my child's teacher teach? So I have simplified all the charts, fuzzy forms, evaluation sheets, observation reports, and confusing grading systems and identified the five main competencies that all teachers need to possess.

Another word for them is *strengths*—just five main teaching strengths—that's all you need to learn about and be able to measure. But those are most important. Without them . . . ? Let's not even talk about that possibility.

Now, I want you to think for a moment and then write down what you think those five strengths are that every teacher has to have.

1. _____

2. _____

3. _____

4. _____

5. _____

Good. Now check your answers against the contents. Did you get some of them right? Most of them? All? That's great!

But no matter how many you got right, now you're involved. You're ready to go. You're not a dream deferrer. You're a let's-do-it-now person.

Look over the contents again, and you'll notice that under each of the five main strengths I mention four parts that make it up. I do this for a reason. By breaking the main strengths into parts, we can understand them better. It's like eating meat—better to cut it up and chew one bite at a time.

Then, at the end of each strength, I've provided a Time to Evaluate section with a look at some real teachers, so you can meet various fine educators—their names have been changed for obvious reasons—working in our schools today. There is also a Teacher of the Year section for your information.

Furthermore, under each of the four parts, or strength components, you'll find a brief explanation in the first paragraph and a lengthier definition under the Details heading. You'll also find an anecdote or real life story, plus a very short section of the Quick Teacher Quiz. As you can tell, I have chopped that up as well. It's easier that way and will stick with you better. You can find the Complete Teacher Quiz in the Appendix, but please read the various explanatory sections first so you'll know what to look for.

Under the heading Does Your Child's Teacher Make the Grade? a simple scoring system for the various quiz parts is provided. Always remember that this is just a guideline for you and not etched in stone. Teaching is truly a life science, a live, fluid, variable process, and we must assess it as such and never be rigid or opinionated.

Next, you will find a segment called Brain Gainers for Your Child. That's a listing of strategies to help bolster and reinforce that particular teacher strength in your child.

Then there's the On a Roll section, which points out ways for you to empower your older child, so your whole family can benefit from your newfound insider knowledge. The final Honor Roll section is merely an outgrowth, the crowning activity, so to speak. Plus, throughout the whole book, I have sprinkled a few personal notes to show you where I'm coming from.

After the five teacher strengths are discussed, we have to look at the rest of the school and the environment in which teachers teach. Again, checklists are provided for you to use, but only as an introductory guide as you assess the overall learning situation in which your child operates.

At the very end you'll find appendixes listing resources that will further your understanding of what makes teachers the quality professionals they are, so, when you finish this book you'll be able to recognize the best teaching traits and get the word out. With your help, even the mediocre teachers still in existence today will improve drastically. You'll see to it; I know you will.

The fact is, it takes all of us—teachers, students, and parents—working together to make our schools first-rate. A strong triangle made up by all participants is required. But really I prefer to make the triangle into a circle. That means one continuous flow of support, goodwill, and achievement among all three segments. As a consequence, everyone in the circle has the chance to take an active part to make the circle great.

But even in the greatest and most dynamic circle there's always one segment, one point, that provides the impetus, the jump start when things slow down, and that's the leader who supports, guides, and leads. That leader is *you*. Yes, you're the captain, the main force, in the winners' circle. So take the helm, please. Do it now.

But wait. There's one more preliminary before we can really get into what teachers know and do and how we can help them, and that section deals with kindness and with giving everyone the benefit of the doubt. Our teachers cannot be tested by a precise yardstick or some other harsh standard against which educators either measure up or it's Hit the road, buddy.

No. Teaching—and I've hinted at this before—is very difficult to do and even more difficult to judge. And outstanding teaching is the hardest of all to assess. So, please, proceed carefully.

CAUTION

Exceptions exist in all fields of expertise. Some doctors are overweight and smoke and yet are outstanding physicians. Some basketball coaches can't hit the backboard, and still their teams win championships. The same is true for teaching. There are excellent teachers who don't possess all of the five crucial strengths or competencies but through some extraordinary gift, talent, or circumstance can instill knowledge into students to a miraculous degree. How lucky we are when our kids encounter such a person!

However, this book isn't about special gifts or unusual great-ness. It's about "regular" teachers who may or may not have an extraordinary teaching talent. This book isn't about the one or two percent of teachers today who are geniuses. It's about all the rest.

Also, it must be made clear from the start that some of these basic yet crucial skills and competencies are very easy to assess. You can do it at home, with a quick phone call or e-mail, or by a brief after-school visit.

To check on other strengths, however, requires spending at least some of your time at school. You can do it in 20 minutes by sitting in on a class and paying attention as an actual observer. Checking to see if your child's teacher makes the grade isn't always easy as pie, but it can and it must be done.

Fortunately, all schools welcome parents. So even with those strengths that are tougher to observe, it's simply a matter of call-ing the school's office a few days or a week ahead and arranging for permission to visit. Then go ahead and spend a little quality time in class with your kid, with this book in hand, and you're through.

Another option: The process can be shortened even more by visiting the class at different times for a few quick minutes. That means making several appointments, but what a thrill. You get a real view, a true picture of your child in action.

Naturally, should your child feel uncomfortable about your presence, just select a different class or a time when your child isn't in school. You're interested in the teaching process, not the individual children.

But no matter which visiting plan you pick, the all-at-once or the-spread-out-over-time one, the fact is that all five crucial teacher strengths can be observed quite accurately in far less time than it takes for one shopping excursion to the mall.

So let's get to it. Here we go. What does it take to be a good teacher? Let's find out once and for all.

Another caution, but I can't say it often enough: The following material is to be taken with a grain of salt. We're dealing with human beings after all. We are human beings ourselves, and therefore we all make mistakes, right? Don't be too harsh in your assessment or too strict in grading the Quick Teacher Quiz. Always remember: When in doubt, do without—criticism, that is.

Teaching well has been called one of the hardest professions and rating teachers is even harder. So tread lightly, please, and learn a lot, and help out where you can, rather than harp on weaknesses. Always keep in mind that the areas of teaching and learning are vast oceans of endeavor. This book is meant just as a dialogue starter, a thought prompter, a simple beginning. It's a collection of steps and strategies that have worked for other parents and will work for you. Remember, education isn't a precise science. It's an art and a craft.

I may be the school doctor, but I'm a general practitioner, not a brain surgeon or kidney transplant specialist. I'm the quick scanner for success, the discussion door opener, the get-you-going gal, the planter of tiny school-success seeds all over the country. It's up to you to take the seeds, water them, and watch them grow. Therefore, in no way is this book a know-all and end-all. Teaching and learning have many aspects, and no one book or author can do all of them justice. Certainly I can't with this book.

But it's a start. And what a start!

Why is teaching so hard?

One reason is that it consists of so many large and small skills and so many complex and simple competencies. You definitely need talent, toughness, and tenacity, the more the better.

Another reason is that teaching is never a finished skill. Whenever you think you've got it down pat, you're proven wrong. With every new group of kids, new problems crop up and more challenges rear their heads.

Also, with our changing population and our constantly fluctuating society, students today aren't like students were a few years ago. Plus, expectations have risen and continue to go up— for student achievement, for school accountability, and for teacher performance.

Teaching is very stressful, and yet society doesn't regard it as such. Sure, an air traffic controller's work or a spine surgeon's career is seen as stressful, but most air traffic controllers would keel over if they had to guide twenty-five planes at once to safe landing.

The surgeon would walk out and quit if the hospital management expected him to perform two dozen complex surgeries at one time.

Yet teachers have the responsibility of meeting the needs of huge numbers of kids every day and simultaneously. I often think that's why teaching has been underexamined and underrated. The task is mind-boggling.

If the truth were ever to come out about how many routine and special tasks teachers carry out each and every day, and if price tags were then assigned to only a few of those activities and duties teachers carry out, their incomes would shoot sky high. So no one ever dares to analyze the problem, because analyzing it would mean having to pay teachers fairly for all the work they do. The end result would be that teachers would have the highest income in the state and the nation, which would bankrupt the various governmental coffers. Better just to overlook the contribution of teachers and underpay them!

While you and I can do nothing to raise teachers' salaries at this moment, we *can* contribute to the public's understanding of just how hard teaching school is. Many people say it's the most difficult job on earth, and those people aren't even teachers. If they were, they wouldn't even try to describe it.

Teaching is indeed the hardest work there is. Let's take it apart step by step and examine it.

Part I: **Before the Lesson**

FIRST | Planning
STRENGTH | and Preparing

Education is a matter of building bridges.

—RALPH ELLISON

A HUNDRED YEARS AGO, teachers had few tools and
resources. A small room with thirty or forty desks (or some
benches and tables) and a lectern or teacher's desk was the
norm. A flag rose in one corner, a map of the United States
curled up in another. Reading, 'riting, and 'rithmetic were the
main subjects, along with religious training. A few tattered textbooks were also available, plus an attendance and grade book in
which teachers recorded who was present on any given day and
what grades they made. In front of the room stood a big dusty
blackboard. Other basics might have included a chart of the
ABCs in cursive and pictures of former presidents.

Teaching back then was quite simple too. There were no
grade level requirements or system-wide curriculum guides.
State-mandated tests did not exist, and teachers were not held
accountable for student progress. Education in those days
involved teaching only those kids who wanted to learn—and
that included a large number, because most students considered
going to school a privilege. School for those kids meant getting

a welcome rest from having to do backbreaking work on the farm or in their parents' stores or baby-sitting younger brothers and sisters.

In short, a century ago education was like TV is for kids today: entertaining, easy, and escapist. It was such fun to file into a cozy classroom, crowd on a bench with other boys and girls, and listen to the teacher tell about Aesop's fables, the lives of our presidents, or how big a piece of apple pie you get when seven friends want to share it with you.

Those were the "good old days" in teaching.

How things have changed. Today's schools are entirely different. They can be huge modern buildings with movable walls, spanking new desks, computers, and security cameras, and cafeterias that resemble the food courts in malls. Or they can be rundown hovels with antiquated facilities and leaking roofs. But no matter how perfect or pitiful schools are today, the looks of a school don't determine what goes on inside the classroom. *A+ teaching can occur in any environment.* The teachers are key. Always have been and always will be.

Like some teachers at present, teachers of the past may have had few facilities but they had what really counted: plenty of power to persuade slow learners to learn. They needed very few skills. All that was required back then was a love for kids and books.

Now, however, in the neglected schoolhouses and even in the most modern facilities, teaching realms have crumbled. Just a decade or two ago, teachers had the power to send misbehaving or uninterested kids out of the room or tell them to stay home.

Today the word *expel* is a no-no. Where can kids be expelled to these days? There's no one at home to keep an eye on them, and the streets are definitely no place for them. So the hands of teachers are tied when it comes to discipline. Meanwhile, their responsibilities have mushroomed. Add to that the fact that our population has changed tremendously, while at the same time our economy demands much better educated workers.

As a consequence, most school systems have set minimum standards, which are going up every year. The federal government also has set a national school testing schedule, and universities everywhere are increasing their admissions standards. Competition for well-paying jobs is getting tougher too.

Teachers are more important than ever. They have to do everything these days: include and inspire all kids; teach all of them at least the required minimum skills, so they can pass regularly given achievement tests; plus develop the good, great, and gifted students at the same time.

What makes this task even more formidable is the fact that all of today's students, no matter what their ethnic or scholastic backgrounds, may resemble those of the past on the outside but are an entirely different group on the inside. They are the "vid kids," children reared with TVs, videos, and other techno toys and tools.

Vid kids are by their nature more knowledgeable and pseudo-adult since from childhood on they have been exposed to many more adult topics than earlier generations. Yet on the other hand they're often less mature, less motivated, and have fewer basic study skills than previous students.

That's obvious when one examines the classrooms of a typical school in the United States. Only a few students are really doing their best. It's estimated that today only a third of all students work hard in class. The rest just vegetate. And that situation gets worse the farther along students move in their grades. Let's face it. Today in any given middle school or high school, the majority of students are in holding tanks and don't do quality work. That's why, more than ever before in history, teacher competencies are crucial. Teachers and only teachers can make the difference in revitalizing our schools and ensuring that all kids reach their potential. Only they can solve the immense challenges of the third millennium. Teachers are indeed key to your kids' success.

Yet teachers, like the modern student body, have varied backgrounds too. Some are well qualified to meet today's challenges. Others, sadly, were trained in the "good old days" methodology and never learned how to teach properly. For that reason, teacher performance can vary drastically from room to room and grade to grade in today's schools. Also, serious teacher shortages have brought staff members, who know little about either the subject or the procedures, into our classrooms.

So what's a parent to do?

Be knowledgeable and helpful. That's crucial. Fortunately there are only five basic teacher skills or competencies. Even better, let's call them *strengths*. They are easy to understand and easy to observe. If they are soundly in place, outstanding teaching will result every time, full-steam ahead learning not only for the few rare and self-motivated students but for all of them.

What are those five basic strengths? What really constitutes A+ teaching? The first is the preteaching skill. In other words; all the preparing and planning that occur before school opens for the year.

1 | Curriculum Goal-Setting

"WHERE IS IT? WHERE IS IT?" twelve-year-old Mike screamed as he tore madly through the house, thumping and bumping everything in his way. Doors slammed, drawers were yanked open, and his stomping downstairs from second floor to basement and back up again was painfully audible.

It was Monday morning, a school day after a long weekend. The previous Friday had been a teacher workday, and Mike's parents had taken him to visit his cousins, who were hyperactive—or so Mike's mother thought in private—and some of that "hyperactivity" seemed to have rubbed off on Mike.

As he came racing past, she stepped into his path: "What're you doing?"

"Move, Mom, please! I can't find it."

"Find what?"

"My library book!"

"Did you look—?" But he was off again on another noisy tear through the house. More slamming sounds, more frustrated exclamations ensued.

"I know one thing," Mom reminded Mike, raising her voice, "you didn't leave it at school."

His response was more racing around.

"Why do you need it?" Mom yelled. By now she was rushing around the kitchen, setting cereal, milk, and bowls on the counter. She had to get ready for work herself, and Mike wasn't the only child in the family.

"Because—because—because—"

"Have you looked at your class calendar?" This was a hand-out giving an overview of basic instructional goals and dead-lines for the year.

At that Mike screeched to a halt, checked a sheet posted on the fridge, and said, "Whew! Right. It's not due till the first of the month."

"Anyway, here it is," his older sister said, pulling the book from Mike's disheveled book bag.

"Keep it," Mike said, and attacked his bowl of Rice Cricklets.

"Saved again by the calendar," Mom said. "I'm going to write your teacher a thank-you note."

The calendar Mom referred to was an overview of yearly learning objectives and reflected work Mike's teacher had done *before* the school year started. First she had gathered the text-books for fifth grade, copies of old state-mandated tests and guidelines, the school system's latest curriculum handouts, and correlated materials. Then she had incorporated all of them into her overall yearly goal and pored over the achievement records of her incoming class. As she studied the various files and glanced at the outlines of the newly adopted textbooks, her master teaching plan slowly began to take shape. She now had her curriculum clearly in mind.

Definition   The curriculum is the course of study offered by a school. Mike's teacher now knew what she was supposed to teach her students this year and approximately where her new group of students was in their abilities and scores. But what a task lay ahead: getting all her students to advance at least one grade level and some of them more than one!

The federal government calls this making "adequate yearly progress," meaning that every child in her class should learn enough to become "proficient." But that wasn't what she had in mind. She wanted her students to exceed basic expectations. By far.

Details   That was the real challenge. That's why planning is so important. During this process Mike's teacher had to

- select the overall goals for the year,
- list all the skills and content to be tested, and
- plan for an instructional overlap.

That meant she taught much more than what the various tests would require, but still she could not leave out a single skill.

She took a deep breath, reheated her cup of tea, and returned to her books and guidelines. After some time, she reached for a stack of legal pads and began to sketch out a more definite plan for the year. Then she divided the overall goals for the various subjects she taught into small and even smaller sections.

Quoting Cervantes, she said: "Rome was not built in a day." And by nightfall, she let out a deep sigh of satisfaction. She had five legal pads filled with ideas.

Her task was tough. By aligning the latest textbooks with her system's curriculum guidelines, and knowing what standardized tests she was going to have to administer, she now had at hand the core contents that she needed to teach, but everything needed double checking. Too often in the past, the local curriculum guide had focused on one area of learning and the textbooks had stressed another, while the standardized tests had emphasized something else entirely.

She returned to her notes, knowing what lay ahead: the creative sequencing of the skills her students needed, the addition of some interesting and enjoyable projects and activities, and the packaging of all her lessons as attractively as possible.

Being the pro she was, she knew every lesson taught had to be as carefully constructed as a miniature sailboat in a bottle. But she wanted her teaching to be preserved, not like a little ship in a dusty bottle on a mantel somewhere but as polished gems of knowledge in the minds of her students. She wanted her work to last forever.

But for now, still in the planning stage, she turned on her computer and typed a rough outline for the year. Fortunately she had time. There were two weeks before school started, and she still had the mandated teacher workdays ahead, during which she would fine-tune her outline and e-mail or call the parents of her incoming class with an invitation to let her know what special highlights she might include. She would compare her outline with those of the most experienced and effective teachers in her school, get more hints and pointers from teachers all across the country via Internet exchanges, and finally tackle the monthly lesson plans that would flow from the yearly plan. Ta–da!

By the time her students arrived in late August, her master plan was firmly in place. After discussing the reasons for the yearly goals with the class, she gave each of her students an out-line of academic tasks to be achieved. She called it their *class calendar* and told the students to take it home.

Meanwhile, in a room across the hall, another teacher's objectives for the year were displayed on the bulletin board in bright letters against a contrasting background. And in yet another room, the teacher had prepared a booklet to read with the students, adding any helpful comments the class made. That turned into a somewhat noisy and messy but meaningful first day for them.

No matter how the overall curriculum goals for the school year are made clear to the learners, the first and most basic skill for any teacher is planning. Lasting learning cannot occur in a vacuum. It has to be fixed in place according to what's expected of the class and then explained to students and parents alike.

QUICK TEACHER QUIZ

Clear signs of this preparing and planning strength need to be readily observable in any classroom. A yearly expectations calendar is as crucial as a blueprint for a house. It doesn't have to be prominently posted, but it should be in evidence in the classroom, included in what students take home as handouts early in the semester, and in what they grasp as the purpose for being in school and what drives their learning process.

And while the overall learning plan is a most important outline, it should be more than just a chart of subject areas to be covered. It should also whet the students' appetite for each segment of the journey, by making them look forward to each new unit and want to participate.

How in the world is that done? A+ teachers know. Follow me to chapter 2, so you'll know as well. But before that, let's quickly quiz for the basics.

This isn't a quiz of the usual kind. It's more like a checklist, but I call it a *yes* list. Let me explain. In this checklist YES indicates where success has already occurred. The blank spaces are just spots waiting eagerly to be checked, as the expected outcome occurs or is observed.

That means the YES lists are ongoing success lists because in the course of the school year these strong points can be encouraged by *you*, so that by the end of the year every teacher in your child's school will have nothing but YES checks beside all the questions on their quizzes. So please, if you can answer YES check the blanks that apply.

YES

_____   1.   Does the teacher provide a handout or calendar of curriculum goals at the beginning of the school year?

_____   2.   Does this handout list the statewide and/or standardized testing dates for the year, plus the latest federal education mandates, if applicable?

___   3. Do you and your child understand this handout?

___   4. Is parent involvement in curriculum planning and enrichment appreciated, and welcome?

___   5. Are class rolls, seating charts, daily and weekly schedules, emergency lesson plans, and special instructions for special students available for substitutes in a clearly marked "emergency" folder?

DOES YOUR CHILD'S TEACHER **MAKE THE GRADE ?**

While exceptions always exist, three or four YES checks are a good starting point. Question number 5 is tricky, unless you are the substitute or know the substitute. But certainly the existence of an emergency folder can be assessed. Just ask the teacher, "Do you have a folder prepared with instructions in case you are ever absent?"

Don't ask that as the first question, but you can certainly work it in during a conference. You might say something like this: My son Mike isn't good with substitutes. He's the type of kid who gets easily upset when there's a change of teachers or routines. So can I tell him not to worry? That even when you're out, there's a folder telling where everybody sits and what the lesson is?

Perhaps you can also ask your child what happened on a day when the teacher was out. Naturally, you never want Mike to turn into a tattletale, but if he should tell you that the sub they had one day was totally stumped, maybe question number 5 doesn't deserve a YES check. Maybe you'd better leave it blank or give it a question mark.

If you have trouble coming up with any YES answers, or if you're unsure about some of the questions, why not call or e-mail your child's teacher? Even better, ask your child's teacher about them at the next parent–teacher conference. There may be many good reasons why you can't put a YES check on one or two blanks.

Rather than focus on anything negative, zoom in on the signs of excellence in this teacher and open the door to a meaningful discussion. In that way, the questions will be a vehicle for school success, which is its purpose.

While you're thinking about the teacher quiz, can you think of other questions about teacher preparation and planning? If so, use the blank lines that follow to write down any other thoughts and ideas you have. Do it now before you forget:

_____

_____

_____

_____

_____

_____

Overall, teachers have the same characteristics as students. They want to excel. So here's your chance to help in this process. Asking teachers a few questions about their planning process and the interconnectedness of their goals, the school's goals, and the local, state, and national educational goals can lead to many great discussions and to much clarification. Teachers truly enjoy explaining the reasons and rationales for their instructional objectives.

Of course, you want to start this process in a warm and wonderful way—with utmost tact—and not in any kind of confrontational manner. How do you do that? Just introduce yourself and say, "My son Mike is in your class this year and I'm so glad."

After that, choose one of the following icebreakers:

- I hope you don't mind, but I've been wondering about . . .
- Excuse me, but could you please explain . . . ?
- I'm sorry, but my child didn't bring home a curriculum calendar or learning plan for the year. Could you please give me one?
- Forgive me, but I still don't understand what the kids will learn this year. Could you please explain again . . . ?

In most areas of this country, teachers get the least respect and the fewest financial rewards. Therefore, please treat them like the most skillful and highest paid surgeons. Teachers don't repair hearts, but they motivate minds—your kids' minds. For that reason, always approach them with the utmost respect and care.

Now, back to that teacher quiz and whatever other questions it caused to pop up in your mind. None of them are any good if they don't benefit your child, right?

Right. Let's focus on the benefits. The more you know about the multitude of skills and the overall content preparation and planning that are involved in teaching these days, the more your son or daughter will gain. And to make sure your child will benefit even more, check out the following brain gainers, pick and choose from them, and put some or all into action. Your focus is on an excellent education for your child and all children and on helping teachers enhance their skills.

- Ask Michelle to create her own yearly academic calendar, using the teacher's outline as a starting point. Then let her extend her own plan for the next two or three school years.

- Remember that joy associated with learning engenders extra effort and will spice up a long academic year. So let her plan for a major fun activity for the weekend after the state tests or other important exams for the year are over.

- Find out what she doesn't understand about the yearly scholastic expectations and explain it to her, more than once if needed.

- Also, reminders can be posted in her room. For example: READ TWENTY LIBRARY BOOKS THIS YEAR. She can change the number as she makes progress.

- Focus on what she considers her weak spots among the yearly objectives and help her overcome them by discussing them with her and providing extra exercises, re-teaching, and added learning.

ON A ROLL

When you're on a roll, you're surging ahead, and it's this energy and excitement you create about the upcoming curriculum that leads Mike to strive for the honor roll.

- Ask him to explain the yearly class objectives to you when you're far away from the home and school environment (for example, on vacation). Is there one activity he can engage in during the holiday that will be a step toward these objectives?

- Ask him to relate the objectives to his short-range academic goals for this year—making all As and Bs, for example.

- Get similar grade-level expectation statements from the "best" schools in the area, state, and nation and then inspire Mike to reach higher and learn more than what his school's plans require. He can read more advanced books or learn more difficult vocabulary words, for example.

- Finally, help him connect the chunk of learning allocated for this school year to his goal for life. Thus you're giving Mike purpose, hope, and, most of all, empowerment.

HONOR ROLL

With your help and support, Mike will indeed be on a roll, and nobody can stop him. Trust me, he'll be aiming to make the honor roll before the year's out. It's only natural that you want to make the honor roll too. That means you becoming the most supportive and teacher-empowering parent in your community. How can you do that? Just think of how best to honor your child's teacher. Could you start her school year off on a wonderful note by sending her a potted plant with a colorful bow? Include a little note that says, *I'm so glad that you're Mike's teacher.*

Now that Mike knows what the yearly goals are, let's get down to brass tacks. Mike's teacher, of course, is way ahead of him. Teachers know that once the overall plan for the work to be accomplished is in place, it has to be executed. That means the classroom has to be organized in such a way that the plans for the year are clearly publicized. Kids can't check a teacher's lesson-plan book, nor do they care to, but they want to see the major units displayed, or hints of them advertised on the bulletin board.

Interest and curiosity rise with exciting peeks at the upcoming lessons; in other words, with previews. That's why TV stations air spots in advance of any major shows. That's why movies feature *teasers*, snippets of upcoming blockbusters, so that excitement builds. The same is true for the classroom. It needs to represent what is being taught currently, and it also needs to foreshadow what's in store for the students.

But that's not all. The classroom also needs to exhibit real sound management. After all, with twenty-five or thirty young bodies in one room, a plan for movement and procedures about moving from learning station to learning station, for example, must be in place. The classroom management plan also needs to be posted, so kids know what to do and how to act at all times. Only then can maximum instruction take place.

How can you tell that sound management is present? Turn the page!

2 | Organization

WHEN TEACHERS ARE WELL ORGANIZED, kids feel secure and confident. A kid needs to focus on understanding the material, not on worrying if teachers know what they're doing. We never want a class to sit back and hold its collective breath wondering if the teacher has his or her act together.

That's why teachers have their hands full, especially at the beginning of the year. They have to plan ahead and make long- and short-range plans. To achieve their long-range goals, teachers need to chop up their yearly curriculum goals into shorter segments, called units, which can cover a semester, a grading period, a month, or a week, depending on the topic.

Definition   The organization of the curriculum includes the act and process of planning what is to be taught and how. In school, organizing the learning content or material means making up an itinerary for an exciting brain journey for the class. That includes fixing up a classroom so the journey is easier. This is an ongoing process. It requires many hours before school starts and demands constant attention at the year goes on.

Details   While the long-range instructional goals are most often decided before the kids show up in the fall and were already covered in chapter 1, short-range goals lend themselves to much more flexibility and creativity. After all, many teacher-created units are like the major meals you plan. Some have to come at Thanksgiving or on birthdays, for instance, while others can be scheduled according to your personal preference.

Similarly, while some units that teachers teach are set or pre-set, many others can be rearranged and offered to students with as much excitement and novelty as possible. In fact, the most flexibility and fun many teachers have deal with how the given subject matter is to be covered. In other words, How do I teach this topic so all kids can learn it quickly and well?

For that, teachers first have to create an environment conducive to learning and studying. Since they have only their classroom—nothing else—it's most important that they arrange this space in such a way that learning flows. And all the basic requirements have to be in place before the kids even start school.

That means teachers have to decide what room arrangement works best. How should they align the desks? How can they make sure they can easily see all the students? How should they set up space for computer work stations? Arrange the bookcases for supplementary books and the filing cabinets for student files? Leave room for basic supplies, such as construction paper and felt-tip markers?

After the floor space is taken care of, it's on to the walls and ceiling. Basic needs there include a bulletin board or wall area for required listings, such as emergency exit routes and safety instructions, school rules, a calendar, hourly schedules, and other important materials. Also, part of the chalkboard must be set aside for daily assignments and homework reminders.

An even larger space in the room is needed for displaying things that catch the students' interest, such as hints about the fascinating units yet to be studied, the outstanding work of previous classes, and of course colorful posters and masterful artwork that bring beauty to the room. What's left? The ceiling! It's a great place for mobiles advertising some of the highlights of the upcoming year or for purely decorative items. Designating which plants to place on windowsills and which prints or stained glass ornaments by famous artists to display is also a matter that needs attention. Overall, the teacher's room should be bright, cheerful, interest-arousing, and inviting. After all, it's the first impression students get when school starts. And, like everyone else, teachers only get one chance to make a good first impression!

The good news is that this teacher strength—organizing classroom space—can easily be assessed. So let's get to it. After a brief look at the room, you can check off the YES list. But before you do that, let me issue this caution:

Never drop in unannounced on any teacher.

Why? It might look to you as if the teacher has free time and you only need a minute. But keep this in mind: Most teachers have *no free time*. Let me explain. What may be listed as PLANNING PERIOD on their daily schedule really means a frantic work period.

Just think: In that one forty-five-minute segment, five hours of preparation have to be crammed, plus getting materials ready for the next day, assuming the teacher teaches five hours; many teach six and have even more duties.

And lunch isn't a good time to drop in on a teacher either. Most teachers work during lunch, supervising their kids—or other kids—or conferring with other teachers, or just calming themselves down after a hectic morning.

So remember: Lunchtime for teachers is work time! Same goes for before-school time and after-school time. You wouldn't think of just dropping in on a neurosurgeon during nonsurgical time, so don't do it to a teacher. They're working hard from the moment they hit the school grounds until they leave the parking lot. No, that's wrong. They work all the time, even at home and on vacation. In the back of their minds, lesson planning and student problem solving never stop.

So whenever you see a teacher just sitting at her desk and doing "nothing," she's probably trying to gather the strength to make it to the rest room. It's a fact that most teachers have no time to answer the call of nature during the day.

That's why on many teacher applications one requirement for the job is having a teacher's kidney: one that can hold from 8 A.M. to 4 P.M. Just kidding, of course, but there's a lot of truth in the saying that some teachers never smile at the end of the day. They're afraid if they do, they might lose control of their bladder.

Equally bad is when it's that time of the month and the teacher can't leave the classroom and take care of what needs taking care of. You know, don't you, that unlike in most jobs, most teachers do *not* get a regular break? And even if some do, they're invariably far removed from the facilities.

Sure, there's a student rest room down the hall, but they're most often very primitive. At any rate, as a teacher would you want your kids to discuss your bathroom habits at lunch? Oh, the tough time teachers have just taking care of their basic needs. The stories they could tell. . . .

QUICK TEACHER QUIZ

As far as evaluating the organizational skills of your child's teacher, just wait for open house at the beginning of the school year. Or make an appointment to discuss Mike's progress and in the course of that discussion let your eyes roam about the room in which Mike spends so much of his time. Then take the second part of the Quick Teacher Quiz.

YES

____   6. Is the classroom clean, neat, and arranged logically?

____   7. Are special rules and procedures posted, along with a map of the school showing which exit to use in case of a fire, tornado, school shooting, or other emergency?

_____ 8. Are work stations set up with computers, paperbacks, or reference books, and is there a place to display students' best efforts?

_____ 9. Is a daily or weekly schedule posted?

_____ 10. Are grading period dates and breaks posted, and are samples of previous student work and previews for upcoming units or otherwise visually stimulating posters displayed?

DOES YOUR CHILD'S TEACHER
MAKE THE
GRADE?

While exceptions always exist, know that three or four checks are a good starting point, but they must include number 7. The safety of our kids is of the utmost importance, and any room that doesn't have the basic evacuation rules and regulations posted must quickly be brought up to snuff. So go back and count your YES checks, keeping in mind that number 7 is crucial.

If you have trouble coming up with other YES answers, or if you're unsure about some of the questions, why not call or e-mail your child's teacher or, better yet, ask about them? There may be many reasons why you can't put a check on some of the blanks. But rather than focus on anything negative, zoom in on the signs of excellence in this teacher and open the door by example to a meaningful discussion. In that way, the quiz will be what it's supposed to be, a vehicle for school success.

While you're thinking about the quiz, can you think of more questions about the way the classroom is arranged and decorated? If so, use the blank lines that follow to write down any thoughts and ideas you have.

_____

_____

_____

_____

BRAIN GAINERS FOR YOUR CHILD

- Help Mike arrange his room with several work stations conducive to learning.

- Buy him a bulletin board, have him write down the basic fire, safety, and tornado drill rules for your house, and post them.

- Set aside space on the fridge and on a wall to display Mike's schoolwork every week. Once a month, the best items get mailed to Grandma.

- Every weekend, ask Mike to make out his weekly schedule, based on school responsibilities and those at home and elsewhere, and post it prominently.

- Discuss with Mike what the consequences are if he doesn't follow the rules at your house, and then carry them out.

ON A ROLL

- Ask Michelle to write a preview for the upcoming units in her class and check with her ever so often to see how close she came.

- Ask her to keep a notebook of three "headlines" describing the key points she has covered in her class so far.

- Connect Michelle through an e-correspondence with a girl her age in another state or a country overseas, so the two of them can exchange news about what units they're studying or will be tackling soon.

- Take Michelle to a used bookstore and let her buy what's missing from the reference shelf in her room. Does she have a dictionary, one in her favorite foreign language, an atlas, a thesaurus, and an almanac?

- Spend twenty minutes one evening a week for a special Show and Tell with Michelle. Ask her to show you what schoolwork she is proudest of and why. Then search your memory, mention similar assignments you did when you were in school, and pass on your best overall study advice to her. That way you'll encourage her to aim for the honor roll.

HONOR ROLL

You want to make the honor roll too, which means being the most supportive and teacher-empowering parent in your community. How can you do that? What about providing your child's teacher with a tiny treat each month, maybe a special soap, a small bottle of hand lotion, three bags of tea with sugar packets, or a few caramel candies? Thanks for being so considerate!

3 | Planning for Differences

MY, HOW STUDENT BODIES HAVE CHANGED! The reason? Whereas once the accepted school policy was just to educate a certain segment of kids—only those who came in wanting to learn—now all kids are welcome and pulled in.

Indeed, these days classrooms hold every kind of student imaginable. Many kids, although the same age, have different academic ability levels, ethnic backgrounds, and interests. Others may be emotionally or physically challenged or exhibit a wide variety of learning styles. Still others may have a limited knowledge of English, be enrolled in English as a Second Language programs, and work way below or way above grade level. In fact, classes nowadays look often like a mini version of the United Nations. That drastic change toward a much greater diversity brings with it many joys and challenges.

Definition   Diverse students may be explained as being dissimilar or different. Teachers nowadays can have their hands full trying to get a grip on all the differences they find from one student to the next. How can I get to a common denominator? they may ask, when the truth is that each student is an exciting puzzle for the teacher to solve.

Details   For that reason every teacher needs to take a deep breath, feel confident of being equal to the task, and then start by taking into consideration all the different levels of achievement and varieties of skills that students in the class possess. Or don't.

Picture a physician having two dozen patients show up in one day, each with a different physical complaint but unable to talk about it. Wouldn't that drive any doctor bonkers? Sure would, yet that's the tremendous challenge teachers face. They have to spend hours delving into the past records of the students, design a lesson plan to meet their various needs, and then assess if those needs are being met.

It's an unending process revolving around this question: Is every student, no matter what his or her needs and previous school experiences are, learning at least one academic year's worth while in my classroom? Or, better, Can I propel my kids on to learn two or three years' worth of knowledge? Every teacher is driven by the hope of making that enormous difference.

For that reason, teachers must use many of sources of information to know what the students' differences are and to make plans for them. These sources include comments and scores from previous teachers and resource teachers if the students have special needs, and the teacher's own diagnostic tests and observations.

Materials on various reading levels have to be obtained, some for the most advanced kids and some for those way behind. Furthermore, depending on the makeup of the class, the teacher has to prepare a few individualized learning folders for the kids with extra-special needs. On top of that, the teacher has to be flexible, because in addition to having such a mix of kids, school calendars change. There are snow days, special assemblies, and other unforeseen schedule changes, all of which require adjusting and fine-tuning.

Besides having the knowledge about what materials and instructional techniques work best with the enormous variety of students in today's classrooms, the teacher also needs to be aware of exceptions and diversities that aren't so obvious. Some students may have a different religion from the rest of the class.

Others live in nontraditional families. Still others come from homes torn apart by death, divorce, or drugs.

So when planning for the multitude of differences that exist in most classrooms today, the teacher focus must be on what can be done to increase the learning potential of each child. What are the possibilities, given the level of skills and abilities?

The possibilities for teachers are endless. There is no ceiling, glass or otherwise, for the dedicated instructor, only the vast blue unending sky and the joy felt in lifting all students up to see it— so they can envision a truly wonderful future for themselves.

Personal Note Of course, teachers aren't all alike either. These days not every teacher is native-born. In many areas of the country there are now such teacher shortages that instructors from foreign countries are imported. That makes kids have to listen extra attentively to their lessons, so they can grasp what's being said.

I know. When I first started teaching in North Carolina in the sixties, my accent was quite heavy. That, however, didn't keep my kids from learning. On the contrary, it was a bonus because it made my students have to really sit up and tune in. The only negative effect appeared one day when I had a substitute. When I came back to school the next day, the sub was quite upset.

"Couldn't please your students at all," she said, "because I don't talk like you. They made me say *vindow* instead of *window* all day long."

I made it up to that sub by paying for her lunch and then had a long talk with the children about always being polite.

Since there's usually just one teacher per class, the differences—should the teacher be from a foreign country, for example—are easily adjusted to. The added bonus here is that the students get an introduction to the whole wide world by having an instructor who's not a native English speaker. And they don't even need air fare!

Meanwhile, the many special student subgroups in a classroom today present a much greater challenge and need plenty of attention. That's where skill and ability really pay off. That's where the teacher's strengths can shine.

QUICK TEACHER QUIZ

Let's pause and check to see how strong your child's teacher is in that area. Can he or she truly meet the needs of today's patchwork quilt of students?

You can assess the teacher's strong points in this area by your conversations, by looking around the classroom, and by checking over the assignments your child brings home. Are there books about various ethnic groups on the reading list? Check on the plans being made for your child—should there be special needs—and by how accepted your child feels if he or she comes from a different background.

Think about the similarities and differences in the kids in your child's room, realize that every student is an individual, and then take the next part of the Quick Teacher Quiz. Here you have to go not only by what you observe in the room and by what you find written in your child's assignment list and textbooks, but also by what kind of feeling you have about this teacher.

Then all you do is check if you can answer YES.

YES

____   11. Is the teacher open-minded and welcoming of
            diverse backgrounds?

_____ 12. Does the teacher help parents of children with special challenges or with nontraditional backgrounds or arrangements?

_____ 13. Is the teacher sensitive to the changes in our society and helpful to all kids whose parents are going through major problems, be they divorce, the death of a family member, substance abuse, or others?

_____ 14. Are multicultural posters and artworks displayed that are representative of all ethnic groups, and are there books and materials from a diverse mix of authors?

_____ 15. Is the teacher sensitive to all cultures and religions by being inclusive rather than exclusive?

DOES YOUR CHILD'S TEACHER **MAKE THE GRADE?** While exceptions exist, know that three or four YES checks are a good starting point. But if you had trouble coming up with any YES answers, or if you're unsure about some of the questions, why not call or e-mail your child's teacher? Better yet, ask your child's teacher about them at the next parent-teacher conference. There may be many good reasons why you can't put a check on some of the blanks. So rather than focus on anything negative, zoom in on the signs of excellence in this teacher and, by example, open the door to a meaningful discussion. In that way, the questions themselves become a vehicle for school success.

And while you're thinking about how your child's teacher deals with student diversity, let me ask you: Can you think of more concerns you have about this topic? If so, please use the blank lines that follow to jot down any extra thoughts and ideas you have.

_____

_____

_____

_____

_____

_____

BRAIN GAINERS
FOR YOUR CHILD

- Get a globe or world map out and, together with Mike, find all the foreign countries he's heard of. Then point out more.

- Ask Mike to name some foreign customs and then ask him to research the origins of one or more of them on the Internet.

- Teach Mike to be nonjudgmental about other people in words and deeds.

- Include your kids' friends and classmates in activities at your house, so they all can learn from you.

- Insist that your kids invite various different classmates throughout the year, even those less popular or smart or cute.

ON A ROLL

- Once Michelle and you talk about all the various nationalities there are, take her to an international festival where she can interact with other kids and taste different meals.

- Point out your favorite foreign language(s) or foreign author(s) to Michelle, and give her a chance to discover her own favorite foreign land or writer.

- Invite her to go with you to hear a lecture by a speaker from another country. Or take her to a traveling art exhibit from a different continent.

- One weekend, take Michelle with you as you participate in a religious observance different from your own.

- Invite people from work who are from foreign countries to your house for a cookout and make sure Michelle gets to meet them. She can ask them about the schools they attended and tell them how hard she's trying to make the honor roll.

HONOR ROLL

You, being who you are, want to make the honor roll too. That means you'd like to be the most supportive and teacher-empowering parent in your community, right? But how can you do that?

Why not consider making your child's teacher feel special by providing breakfast one morning? It could be a cheese Danish or a ham biscuit, something to microwave later in the lounge and eat at coffee break. Maybe you can find out what state the teacher is from, or what foreign foods the teacher likes, and then get something that hits the spot.

Or take a surprise—a snack or some fruit, which teachers especially love. Maybe a little basket of strawberries or cherries, plums or a pear, dropped off on your child's teacher's desk tomorrow morning?

4 | Variety of Activities

NOT ONLY HAVE STUDENT BODIES CHANGED enormously over the years but teaching methods have as well. Where once the range of instructional skills and teacher tricks went from reading to the class to having students recite back to the teacher what they had learned, we now have a whole menu of options for the savvy teacher to choose from. We call this *instructional variety.*

Definition   *Variety* is the quality of having different forms. In the classroom that means, Is the teacher able to find and use all kinds of exciting teaching and learning opportunities?

For example, there is teacher-centered teaching, which can be divided into whole-class instruction, small-group instruction, and one-on-one instruction. Often new material is introduced first to a whole class by a lecture and then taught or retaught to smaller groups.

Meantime, during this process, the teacher has to decide on how long to lecture, how much time to devote to discussion, and what kind of questions to use:

- Those that add new information?
- Those that are open-ended?
- Those that get students deeply involved in discussion?

Another method of delivering knowledge to students is a more student-centered teaching style. This may include:

- group work,
- team learning,

- peer teaching,
- group presentations,
- individual presentations, and
- independent study.

Details Obviously, there are many instructional methods for today's teachers to learn and then to use. While a student-centered approach sounds easier than straightforward lecturing, it's more difficult because the teacher has to make many crucial choices. For instance, in group work, how large should the groups be? Should students group themselves or should the teacher group them—and how? According to achievement levels? In such a way as to include different study skills or learning styles? Or base the groups on their stated topics of interest? Should the groups represent—as much as possible—a great mix of male and female students from various ethnic and/or religious backgrounds? Decisions, decisions. Which will most easily maximize learning?

Much depends on what kind of class is being taught and what subject matter is at hand. Yet in almost every subject, straight teacher lectures should be short segments and not take up the whole hour.

But that's not all. The teacher has to keep track of each group's progress. Too much time in group work leads to wasting precious minutes, while not enough time can lead to frustration. And certain types of student personalities should never be in the same group, lest chaos erupt.

Another sticking point is splitting up the learning tasks among the members of the various groups to prevent shirking or hotdogging. Shirking occurs when, in a group of five kids, for example, one does everything while the other four twiddle their thumbs. Hotdogging means that, in a group of five, one student takes over, while the rest are left with nothing but the boring busywork.

Then, after the groups of kids working together on an assignment are all set, the presentation needs to be considered. Do the students self-select when they want to give their report, or does the teacher assign the order of presentation? And what do you do if, on the day of group report, several kids are absent?

Teachers have to go through these steps and considerations for every class. If they teach five or six classes, major headaches loom on the horizon. Often, what works best for teachers is a series of activities that include elements of various instructional strategies. Sometimes this series can be completed during one hour. Other times it will take several days to go from an introductory lecture to small-group instruction, to peer teaching, to group work projects, and to independent study. But really outstanding teachers know how to mix it up during the course of the unit so that student interest remains high.

Now, you wonder, How great is my child's teacher in this category? How varied is the teacher's approach? Here you're in luck. You can easily check on that strength simply by asking your child several days in a row, What did you do in school today? How did you learn what you did? What was the most fun? Don't let Mike get away with just shrugging his shoulders. If he does, insist on some details about his day. Ask: Did you listen to the teacher all day? Did you move your desk around at any time? Did you get to work with a friend or classmate?

Also, by checking Mike's homework, looking over his notebook, and helping him work on his various class projects, you'll get a good idea of the different activities taking place in Mike's room. In addition, check Mike's learning plan or yearly calendar. It will give you an insight into the many diverse learning opportunities Mike's teacher has scheduled. Get ready to marvel at the tremendous variety of teaching strategies being used, and then check off the next part of the Quick Teacher Quiz.

QUICK TEACHER QUIZ

YES

___ 16. Does the lesson plan vary during the week?

___ 17. Is group work included as well as team learning, pair learning, and computer research?

___ 18. Do students have a choice of activities?

___ 19. Are teacher lectures requiring note-taking no longer than 15 to 30 minutes?

___ 20. Are student-created products and projects, videos, skits, and plays, and written and oral book reports scheduled several times a year?

DOES YOUR CHILD'S TEACHER **MAKE THE GRADE?** This teaching strength is very important because kids get bored easily; variety spices up their lessons. Therefore, while exceptions exist, know that three or four YES checks are a good starting point, especially if numbers 16 and 18 are among them.

It's very important for teachers to liven up their assignments. These days kids tend to have shorter attention spans than in the past. Since teachers cannot change society except by changing one student at a time, they must help their kids to have positive feelings toward themselves, their class, and the subject matter.

Keeping that in mind, teachers will want to show off all their various teaching skills, just like musicians present their best work and actors give their best performance. Yet even the most versatile teachers sometimes offer nothing but straightforward lectures to class after class for some reason. Whatever the reason might be, I don't know, but I'd sure want to find out.

If you have trouble coming up with any YES answers in this category, or if you're unsure about some of the questions, why not call or e-mail your child's teacher? Better yet, ask your child's teacher about them at the next parent-teacher conference. Maybe the subject at hand can only be taught by teacher talk. Rather than find fault, zoom in on the signs of excellence in this teacher and, by example, open the door to a meaningful discussion. That way, the checklist questions will be a vehicle for school success.

While you're thinking about instructional variety, do you have more questions? If so, use the blank lines that follow to write down any thoughts and ideas you have, before you forget:

_____

_____

_____

_____

Your own questions will lead you to answers that will not only help you understand teachers better but will encourage you to empower your son and your daughter to become constantly smarter in school and in life. How? Just go on to the simple brain gainers below and put them to use.

BRAIN GAINERS FOR YOUR CHILD

- Have Michelle and a friend study together regularly in a study-buddy system.
- Help extend her attention span with a kitchen timer, and show her how to vary her daily and weekly schedules.
- Establish a learning routine for Michelle that includes her relatives. Just ask yourself, What are the scholastic strengths among the various members of my family? Link Michelle up with them by phone or Internet.

- Plan for a short learning review time every day, in the car on the way to school or over breakfast.

- Praise Michelle for every improvement she makes in listening carefully to the teacher and in taking excellent notes.

Every little effort you make to empower Michelle to "own" her learning will help her get closer to making top-notch grades and getting on the honor roll this term. While there's no guarantee that she'll definitely make it, these suggestions will surely help her toward that goal, step by step. Same goes for Mike.

ON A ROLL

- Discuss and practice the different learning techniques with Mike. One day after school, read a paragraph to him and have him take notes. Next day, let him work alone. On a third day, pair him off with his sister or another classmate and watch how they tackle studying.

- Encourage Mike to interview older students, such as highly motivated high school and college kids, to snag their best study hints.

- Take Mike with you on a visit to a nearby college and let him observe college students in the process of studying on campus, in a classroom, in the library, and in the computer lab.

- Help Mike make the best use of flash cards, highlighting pens, mnemonics, key words, and fun study techniques.

- Let Mike decide how he wants to handle homework— after you provide a desk, a quiet atmosphere, and at least an hour and a half of uninterrupted time for him.

HONOR ROLL

No doubt about it. You want to make the honor roll too, by being the most supportive and teacher-empowering parent in your community. As you know, you only have about twenty years to rear Mike and Michelle in such a way that they can reach their potential and become productive members of society. So what can you do? How about just one thing: post an HONOR OUR TEACHERS bulletin board?

But that's too much work, you say. No, it isn't. All you need do is get the principal's permission, find a local store to donate a bulletin board, and have Michelle or Mike help you mount it on the wall space the principal assigns you.

And then—by working with the student government or the school newspaper staff—post a snapshot and brief bio about each teacher. Above that bulletin board, put in big letters, HONORING OUR OUTSTANDING TEACHERS.

5 | Time to Evaluate

NOW IT GETS REALLY INTERESTING. To read and think about the signs of quality teaching is one thing, but to be able quickly and easily to observe them in reality and spot them in any classroom in the world, that's another thing. But that's what you'll be able to do soon. How? By meeting some teachers who stand out. Then, after I introduce them to you, see for yourself if you can now detect some signs of their teaching strengths, skills, and competencies.

Afterward, let's find out if you agree with my ratings of "good teacher, better teacher, best teacher" or not. For that's the point here. I want you to be able to look at any teacher, no matter where, and spot their greatness right away, but so far only in one area: planning and preparing.

So here we go: Please meet three outstanding educators. Of course, I'm only presenting a small slice of their teaching talents in this section, so forgive me if the meeting is short. Yet trust me: You'll have no trouble in detecting the signs of quality teaching.

GOOD TEACHER Lynda Bradley, a first-year teacher, is filled with enthusiasm. It springs from her like a fountain, evident in the way she talks and walks and especially in the way she throws herself into the only job she has ever wanted—teaching elementary school.

From childhood on, Lynda loved school. It helped that her favorite aunt was a teacher and always took her along on the work days before school officially opened. So from first grade on, Lynda found the atmosphere in a freshly cleaned school building exciting. And oh, how she liked looking through the folders her aunt kept on the various curriculum segments she taught! It didn't take long for that to rub off on Lynda. From fourth grade on, she started making up her own pretend lesson plans. But back then she didn't teach anyone besides her collection of dolls and stuffed animals, whom she used to line up on her den floor and read to. Later, she prepared actual worksheets for her toy pupils and filled them in herself, so every "student" got an A+. Then she glued all the A+ papers on her bedroom wall—a definite no-no. But her mom's screams didn't deter Lynda from her dream.

In high school she excelled every time she was asked to give an oral presentation. Her many hours spent reading out loud to her stuffed animals paid off. Also her cheerleading experience helped to reinforce her outgoing personality. And when Lynda went off to the state university and started majoring in education, she actually managed to get a long-standing rule changed.

It was the policy of the teacher training program in which she enrolled not to send student teachers back to the schools from which they graduated. But Lynda made an appointment with the dean of the School of Education, brought in the old A+ report cards from her first toy class, and persuaded him to change the rule. And ta-da! She was back in her school, this time as a teaching intern.

She didn't come alone. She brought with her all the lesson plans she had either observed her aunt teach, or had been taught, or had observed her favorite teachers carry out.

Of course, Lynda couldn't use them exactly the way she had seen those plans in action. But by going through them, she picked out the best ones, applied them to the curriculum guidelines she'd been given, and went on to decorate her room with a fall theme.

Since she had such a wealth of materials, she weeded out what wasn't relevant but yet included different activities for each unit. Remembering her stuffed teddy, her Barbie doll, her toy Scotty dog with one leg missing, and the fuzzy little elephant her brother had run over with his bike, she saw her students as little individuals ranging from bratty to brainy and from scruffy to scrupulously reared and prepared a detailed plan for the whole spectrum of kids that exists today. She anticipated that some of her students would be good old-fashioned learners but that the majority of them would be challenging in some way.

I can't wait, Lynda said, to anyone willing to listen.

The day before the students came, she woke up in the middle of the night worrying if teaching her own class would be as easy as she imagined. What if I'm not ready? she wondered. What if teaching isn't the piece of cake I'm hoping it is? It wasn't, but Lynda's enthusiasm saw her through.

And what a fine year she had. Every child learned, and every parent beamed. Just one look at Lynda's enticing classroom convinced them their kids had an exceptional teacher, plus—

Uh-oh, sorry. Lynda's got to run. She just found out that another teacher had a bad day and wants to share some of her best lesson plans with him.

BETTER TEACHER

Across the parking lot from Lynda's school is a high school with a classroom that's totally different from Lynda's. And that goes as well for the teacher whose domain this room is.

First to the room. It's sparsely decorated but very neat, with all the desks in straight rows and facing the front of the room. Magic Marker lines are drawn on the floor where the desks are supposed to be, just in case they should be jostled out of order. Also the chalkboard has the various sections precisely marked off, as to where the daily assignments will be written, the homework will be posted, and other important messages will be displayed. Everything's super neat and done just so.

The room is freshly painted in a color not seen anywhere else in the school, leaving one to believe that the teacher either got special permission to have the room decked out in light green, rather than the institutional beige seen all over the building, or more likely, spent one weekend himself painting his classroom with paint he picked out and paid for out of his pocket.

At any rate, the room stands out, and so does Mr. LaMont Jones! He too is quite different from the rest of the school staff. A former Green Beret, he is tall, has a neat black beard and very short black hair, and always dresses extremely well. He walks with purpose and has a way of directly looking at his students that disarms them.

LaMont had already spent twenty years in the army when an old back injury forced him to retire from his military career. But the army's loss was the school system's gain. And in no time he started his second career, bringing with him all the qualities that made him such an outstanding soldier—order and organization among them.

LaMont didn't know anything about teaching, but he knew that students are impressed by a well-prepared teacher—because having a superior who had his act together to the nth degree had always impressed *him*.

So he got a copy of the textbook three months before school started and went over it, keeping the curriculum goals in mind. He underlined the skills he was supposed to teach and planned out the whole year's work. Then he devoted one legal pad to each unit, which he filled neatly with additional notes. He included three levels of achievements in all his notes: easy, harder, and most advanced. With those three categories, he decided, he'd be prepared for whatever skills his future students would bring to the class.

Next he surveyed the rest of the social studies department at his school and the five others in the district to find out what, besides lecturing, he could incorporate into his lesson plans.

Since LaMont was exposed to many different people while he was in the military, having gone overseas on seven different occasions, he felt that no matter how varied his students might turn out to be, they wouldn't present him with a problem he couldn't handle.

Still, he got out another bunch of yellow legal pads, labeled each one with a term currently in use in educational circles, such as *attention deficit disorder, hyperactivity, limited English proficiency,* and so on. Then he went back through his curriculum plans and filled in a variety of activities for each "student characteristic" on his special legal pads.

But man! It got complicated. So he bought several three-ring binders, one for each unit, tore out his basic lesson plans, punched holes in the sheets, and filed them. Then he sorted through his preliminary lesson plans on the three skill levels and added extra notes and varied activities for those students who might present special problems.

OK. He waited for his first class to begin while reading a best-seller on the lives of the presidents. LaMont was now well prepared overall, but he knew that little-known anecdotes would spice up his talks.

What wasn't in the history book would stick with his students more than what was.

Fact is, LaMont considered the fleshing out of his lessons among his most important prep moves. When he found a little nugget, he marched across the hall and asked the teacher there, Rosa Cruz: "Do you know which president was the shortest and weighed the least?"

It turned out to be James Madison, who was five feet four inches tall and weighed 100 pounds.

BEST TEACHER

Mrs. Cruz laughed, and said, "No, I didn't know the answer to that one," but she made herself a note. Nothing to do with learning was ever lost on her.

She was a short woman, a little overweight, with dark straight hair that was thinning. She walked with a limp that was noticeable only when she hurried, so most students never saw it. Plus, once she fixed you with those dark eyes of hers that were so penetrating and expectant, students worried only about coming up with the correct answer. To disappoint Mrs. Cruz would have been unthinkable.

And yet, Rosa didn't consider herself to be an expert on anything, least of all teaching. On the contrary. Having taught for over twenty-five years, she felt that she was just now picking up on the finer points. One reason was that, up to this point, she had still had her two children at home. As a divorced woman, she was almost totally responsible for them, so the best she could do was just teach one day at a time.

Now that both kids were in college, Rosa could really devote herself to her work. An avid reader, she never stopped planning her lessons. All year round, whatever she read that was of interest, or whatever she heard about or had a chance to see in movies or presented on stage by the drama department of the local college, went into her vast collection of potential lesson plans. Her mind was a rich reservoir.

Naturally as teacher of English, Rosa was helped by her abiding love for literature, plus an interest in travel. Knowing that there was always so much more to learn in her field, as new writers constantly emerged, she kept a stack of books she was reading on hand. She knew that every book ever written represented the essence of the author in some way.

She viewed her students similarly. In them was the essence of what they *could be*, and it was her job to bring that out. Since she was an immigrant herself, she had experienced in her own life how far education could propel her. Now, with her kids in college, she saw firsthand how much further kids today could go. It became her duty to open doors for all her students, to open those doors wide!

It started with her classes. From the moment her students entered her room, she would take them on the most fascinating journey of their lives. Her curriculum plans were masterpieces in progress, which never stopped. There wasn't a trip to the mall or a snippet she read in the newspaper that might not find itself inserted into a lesson.

Rosa was so well prepared she could have taught for a month without looking at a lesson plan, but that was only because she spent so much time preparing. Yet her outlines, notes, and activities were never the same year after year. Older brothers and sisters couldn't just pass their notebooks on to the younger kids in the family, because every year Rosa revamped her plans, kicked out anything that wasn't cutting edge, and added whatever was hot.

English is a living language, she said, and her lesson were living too—something to prune the deadwood from while coaxing out ever more beautiful blossoms.

And so all her students thrived.

Wow.

YOUR CALL

Now it's time for you to make up your mind. Which of the three teachers you have met so far do you think is the best?

Can't decide? Then just for a moment, pretend you're a judge instructed to determine which of the three should receive a special award. Now who has your vote for good, better, or best? You will learn the correct answer in the last chapter.

TEACHER OF THE YEAR

Almost every school selects a Teacher of the Year (TOY) and frequently the various school Teachers of the Year in a given school system are entered in a competition or an interview session held by a committee of administrators, school board members, and community representatives, after which one teacher is selected as the whole system's Teacher of the Year. This tremendous teacher then advances to the district competition and later to the state and national levels to be rated, judged against other candidates, and found to be tops.

This process is never totally fair. Politics matters, as does who makes the nomination and how many fellow teachers are one's friends. Sometimes winning the TOY designation is due to a pity vote because an especially hardworking teacher has had a series of bad luck. Other times, it's a rousing round of applause for the extraordinary work the teacher has done. Therefore, getting named Teacher of the Year can be an unfair judgment or a well-deserved one. I know all about the process, and its positive and negative aspects, having been Orange County Teacher of the Year, then called "Outstanding Young Educator," and having represented that system at the state level.

Oh, what a humbling and exciting process it is to be recognized by your peers. It's heartwarming, even if you don't become the nation's "Top Teach." In fact, it's truly an opportunity to grow and become the best teacher you can be.

For that reason it's important for you to learn who the Teacher of the Year is at your child's school. No matter how unscientific the selection process may be, this particular man or woman does have something special that makes for outstanding teaching.

What is that quality? Often it's just extra energy, dedication, and creativity, although many more special teaching traits may be in evidence, such as attention to detail, duty, and a dash of daring. This teacher doesn't always wait for the latest mandate but soars ahead. And in every case the teacher will be strong.

So let's find out who last year's TOY is at your child's school. Arrange a short meeting and see for yourself what makes this teacher so special. Then, as soon as you get home, jot down your observations below. What impressed you most about the Teacher of the Year? Can you encourage that same quality in other teachers?

_____

_____

_____

_____

_____

This concludes the section on Planning and Preparing in teaching. Where this strength exists, students will walk into a great classroom. And then what? Then comes the thrilling part—the actual lesson.

Part II: During the Lesson, Part 1

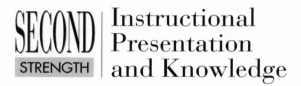

SECOND
STRENGTH

Instructional Presentation and Knowledge

Only the educated are free.

—EPICTETUS

ERRICK AND EBONIE are like many a brother and sister: They often squabble with each other, but underneath they're very devoted. When it really counts, they come through for each other.

Case in point: It's a Wednesday morning before school at their house. Even though Ebonie is a tall twelve-year old and usually good about everything, she's frazzled to the max.

No, *no, no!* she keeps fussing, while trying on different outfits and tossing them back on the bed, pitiful rejects.

Nothing suits her this morning. Nothing pleases her, especially not the happy whistling coming from Errick, whose door bursts open seconds later. Out he strolls, with his hair brushed just so and his khakis creased, but not too much. He's singing now, and his T-shirt is tucked in with a flannel shirt over it like a casual-Friday blazer.

By now Ebonie is screeching from frustration. "Shut up!"

Even though she picked out a great outfit the night before and it was, like, perfect, the top has short sleeves, and she can't find a matching jacket. One look outside told her she'll need something to cover up. Brrr. Back she dives into her closet and her dresser, whose drawers look like off-price sales tables with everything jumbled to high heaven.

Meanwhile, Errick's already going downstairs, two books under his arm. On top of the books nestles his term paper, typed neatly with footnotes. It's clipped inside a clear plastic folder to keep it from getting rained on.

Not that it's raining already, but there are clouds. Plus, the plastic will keep the fingerprints of the other kids off. You know how everyone always wants to look at Errick's stuff before he turns it in? He sure doesn't want smudges on his work, no sir.

Now Ebonie has found some pants she likes but hates the top that's supposed to match it. And where is the belt? The pants are kind of loose, which is good, but without a belt? Well, maybe another top—No, a sweater. I know, the one with the blue stripe. Yikes, it's got these picks on it—Mama! Mama!

Her mother yells from the kitchen, "I can't hear you."

Errick says, "It's nothing, Mama. Just the usual Ebonie mess."

He gets his backpack, which sits waiting under the table in the hall. He packed it the night before with everything he needs and only took two books upstairs with him. He read the chapter they're on and the next one just so he'll know what's going to crop up in chemistry class today. Also, he skimmed over his term paper. That teacher! He really likes for his students to spout off about their research as he calls each one of them to the front and takes up their work.

Not to fret: Errick's ready. With the last name of Adams, he usually gets called on first.

By the time Ebonie scurries down for breakfast out of breath, it's time to leave for school if she wants to ride with her brother. Some juice in a paper cup and a hot Pizza Pop, and she's out the door.

Except Ebonie is screaming. "Where's my spelling book? My lunch money? My hair!" She's gotten only half of it braided. *"My math homework!"*

"It's right here in your math book," Mom says, hoping to calm Ebonie down.

No such luck. "That's only the answers," the girl wails. "We're supposed to do it the long way and show every step—"

"This it?" Errick is holding a bunched-up sheet he fished out of the trash can.

That evening Errick comes in carrying an erasable bulletin board. "Women!" he snorts.

"LaKeisha dump you?" Ebonie asks.

"No way. I'm talking about you. Ran across your teacher in the mall today and she says it's now or never, so follow me." He climbs up to his sister's room, hammers the bulletin board on the wall, whips out a marker, and lists the following:

> Homework—every subject
>
> Books
>
> Backpack
>
> Outfit
>
> Lunch money or lunch

Then he turns to Ebonie, who's been watching him.

"What else?"

"What're you doing?"

"Getting you organized," he says. "Oh, yeah." He writes down *doodads.*

"What's that?"

"All those things you like to put in your hair. Beads, ribbons, other junk. Now listen. We both know, ever since Dad died last year, Mom's been having a hard time. So you're not going to add to it, got it?"

Ebonie nods, wide-eyed.

"From now on, every evening I want you to get your mess together before you turn on TV or talk on the phone or whatever. Check each item off on this list. Tomorrow morning I want you up and dressed and downstairs when I get there. Do you understand? No more wasted time!"

6 | Materials on Hand

WASTED TIME! That's exactly what teachers want to avoid. After all, schools deliver instructional presentations and knowledge, and nothing is supposed to get in the way. But if five minutes are wasted every hour, and you multiply that by the number of class hours taught per day, and then multiply that by the days per week, the weeks per school year, and so on. . . .

You get the picture, don't you? In school every precious minute counts. And students like Ebonie can be an obstacle to that. Thank you, Errick, for straightening her out. Now Ebonie has her act together at home *and* at school.

Back to A+ teachers. Did you think that since the teacher has his or her curriculum goals and room ready, rules posted, and students' strengths and weaknesses analyzed—as in our earlier chapters—that everything is ready to go? "What else is there besides teaching the lessons?" you ask.

Exactly. Now theoretically the teacher can teach, but even that process involves many steps. First is having everything at hand, as Errick tries to do. For a moment, think of what you need to do your job: perhaps a desk, files, and a computer, if you work in an office. Or perhaps your cash register and a pen, if you work in a store. Or some ingredients, such as flour, yeast, unsaturated oil, and eggs, if you're a cake baker, plus sifters, rolling pins, tins, and pans, in addition to an oven and a cooling rack. That adds up to ten basics.

As a teacher you need many more materials, perhaps hundreds of them, and they change from day to day and often from hour to hour.

Definition   Teaching materials can be described as the tools and odds and ends all teachers need to do their work. Let's start with the basics: a roll book, lesson plan book, seating chart, the teacher's edition of textbooks, and notes, curriculum guides, and yearly outline.

Teachers also need equipment such as a calculator, overhead projector, computer and printer, a TV with a VCR and appropriate videos, and a tape recorder with learning tapes and blank ones.

In addition, there must be sets of textbooks for all the students and quite a few on various reading levels, many folders— some of them for portfolios, others for test results, parent notes, and memos—and handouts such as work sheets, study outlines, and review guides. Plus a classroom library, extra books to ensure diverse authors are included, and reference books such as encyclopedias, dictionaries, maps, and thesauruses. Don't overlook posters, charts, and graphs and naturally all the desks, tables, chairs, and file cabinets.

Then it's on to other important items: pencils, crayons, pens, felt-tip markers, masking and clear tape, scissors, rulers, glue, construction paper—stacks of it—and poster paper in the school colors and others, as well as letter stencils, paper clips, straight pins, staplers and staples, thumbtacks. . . . The list goes on and on.

Details   None of those supplies are any good if the teacher doesn't establish a quick routine as to how the students are to enter the room, get their backsides into their seats and their minds on the lesson, and have their own materials ready. That's tough.

As a teacher you're not only responsible for the various items being on hand and the equipment being workable—and we all know how often things can break or be "lost"—you also have to instruct your students on how to handle supplies properly, and put them back without breaking or tearing them and also to bring their own appropriate school tools to class, settle down quick as a wink, and be ready to go.

For that the teacher needs to establish a quick routine that works, depending on the type and age of the students. And what works early in the year may not work later. So the first routine may need to be varied as the year proceeds.

But no matter what happens, it has to take place quickly. Every extra second wasted on the opening routine, which includes not only the kids getting settled but also making sure their physical needs are met, attendance is taken, and all eyes are on you, eats into actual teaching time. So this task is most important and challenging, because it demands even more. Hard to believe, but besides having all the materials ready—the teacher's and the students'—a method must be found to quickly hand out the day's work sheets and, even more crucial, to explain the day's lesson in such a manner that every child understands the purpose of the hour's instruction. There's an added twist—to engage the child's interest in the task at hand—and all in just minutes. It's mind-boggling.

QUICK TEACHER QUIZ

Let's find out how your child's teacher handles this monumental task. How expertly does he or she get all the tools—the human ones and the machinery—up and cranking? Do we even dare to evaluate this performance?

Sure, but let's do it generously. Before we start, there's one problem. This starting-class strength is a skill you can't observe as an outsider. In this case, you have to be there. So please, make an appointment with your child's teacher and ask if you can observe the start of class one day at the teacher's convenience.

After the teacher tells you when to come, walk quietly into the room, sit in the back, and get out your pen or pencil. As soon as the bell rings and the kids come streaming in, look over this part of the Quick Teacher Quiz and check what you can.

YES

____ 21. Are books and other materials ready and handouts issued promptly?

____ 22. Do all students get their textbooks, paper, and pencils out quickly?

____ 23. Does the teacher quickly explain what the lesson is about, why and how it will be taught, and what materials will be used, and are key points written on the board?

____ 24. Is attendance taken during the introductory comments and explanations?

____ 25. Does this opening-class process take less than five minutes?

DOES YOUR CHILD'S TEACHER
MAKE THE GRADE ?

As we said, please be generous when grading this category.

You know why. Goodness! There can be many times when beginning a class doesn't go as planned and takes longer than five minutes. But there has to be a reason: late buses, many children out sick or returning from having been sick, maybe Caitlin upchucking in the back of the room. Otherwise, all systems should be go in a very short time in every classroom in this country.

Now look at your list of YES checks, please. The most important one is number 24. The teacher must take roll, no matter
what else is going on in class, even during an emergency. No,
not even—*especially* during an emergency, every child needs to
be accounted for.

Of course, taking roll can be done by a quick scanning of the
room or orally, with the teacher calling each name, but atten-
dance-taking is an absolute must. Schools have to keep records
of our kids' presence.

Therefore, after counting your checks, know that three or
four checks are good, but only if they include number 24. The
next most important item is number 23. Kids who know what
they're going to learn, why and how they're going to learn it,
and have reminders posted on the board become partners in the
education process.

If, however, you had trouble coming up with any YES answers,
or if you're unsure about some of the questions, why not do the
following? Call or e-mail your child's teacher. Even better, ask
your child's teacher about them at the next parent-teacher conference. There may be a reason why you can't put a check on
some of the blanks. And again, rather than focus on negatives,
please zoom in on the signs of excellence in this teacher and be
the one to start a meaningful discussion. Then the quiz will be a
vehicle for school success, and that's its purpose.

While you're thinking about class startup materials, can you
think of more about this topic? If so, use the blank lines that follow to write down any other thoughts and ideas you have.

_____

_____

_____

_____

_____

BRAIN GAINERS FOR YOUR CHILD

- Carry out a quick check of Ebonie's study area. Does she have everything—paper, pencils, pens, notebooks, coloring pencils, felt-tip markers, dictionary, atlas, almanac, thesaurus, reference materials, and access to a personal computer?

- Fill in what's missing. How much fun it is to go shopping with her for cool school tools!

- Time her. Can she start doing her homework in five minutes or less? If not, help curtail her delaying tactics.

- Sit down and flip through her textbooks with her to provide an overview of all the wonderful material she's going to study this year.

- Help her check out and read a library book every week and ask her to summarize the key points.

ON A ROLL

- Ask Errick to tell you every day what the main purpose or specific goal of his favorite class was.

- Help Errick to develop an appreciation for his *least* favorite class by delving into the subject matter together at home, laughing about it, and learning more about it.

- Ask Errick to compare the makeup of his textbooks by examining the contents tables, indexes, illustrations, chapter headings, and overall designs and then rate his books.

- Teach Errick how first to skim a chapter by reading only the topic sentences of the paragraphs and the summaries, and then to slow down and read all the pages.

- Ask Errick to rate his own home study system and insist that he include some planned downtime when he just sits and lets the minutes drift away aimlessly. Just as his body needs rest, so does his brain.

HONOR ROLL

As both Ebonie and Errick now strive for the honor roll, you want to make the honor roll too. In your case, that means being the most supportive and teacher-empowering parent in your community. How can you do that?

Think about teachers' salaries and for a few minutes compare them with those of other professionals. It won't take you long to realize how underpaid our teachers are. Many have to hold second jobs, not only during the summer but also on weekends. Teachers who have kids find themselves especially strapped. Just one example: Have you visited a high school recently and compared the teachers' parking lot with that of the students? If so, you will have noticed that teachers drive the clunkers while the students drive the hot wheels.

Why not get a teacher discount system going in your area? Work with the PTA, other parents, or just by yourself. See if you can't get at least one store or restaurant to offer teachers 20 percent off on their purchases. Then have the art club at your child's school design the discount coupons you snagged, print them, and hand them out. Feel the power that's in you. You're empowering educators by crystallizing the appreciation of your community!

7 | Getting and Staying on Task

ALL RIGHT, NOW, HERE WE GO. The tricky opening-class routine is over with. Pretend you're the teacher. It's five minutes into the class and you've done well! You've issued all the books and papers, accounted for the kids, explained the goal for the hour of instruction ahead, and all eyes are on you. Great. What's next? Isn't the easy part of teaching about to begin?

What easy part? There are no easy parts in teaching, and there's certainly nothing easy about what's next, which is getting the students on task and keeping them there.

Definition In school the word *task* refers to a piece of work or on activity assigned by a teacher. That translates into a fairly simple routine if the task is easy to do. But most school tasks are taxing because they involve new material.

New material, which continues to get harder each day, is what makes keeping the kids' attention on the task at hand so tough. So after the teacher has explained what will be learned, the real job begins: the learning itself.

Details I know: In your assumed role as a teacher for the moment, you're already moaning because you can envision a day of panic. The new books you ordered for this class didn't come in. The printer was out of toner. The buses ran late, meaning only a third of the class showed up. And you're having the worst sore throat of your life. Now what?

Don't panic. There will be days like that, of course, though most days don't have *that* many things go wrong. Yet even on good teaching days, you'll still have to be on your toes constantly. Why?

Because there are so many things the teacher has to juggle at one time. In truth, when teachers hear the word *multitasking*, they can only laugh. That word doesn't even begin to describe the various things they do simultaneously each and every day. Not even *megamultitasking* is an adequate term for their work.

Only five minutes into class, teachers would already be breathless if they weren't the pros they are. And as we said, they're only out of the starting gate. Now begins the real race.

First, teachers have to make sure the assignment for the day has been understood by each student and has been explained in such a manner that each learner can get started right away. For a moment, picture yourself corraling twenty-five strange men and women—all around age forty—in the mall and trying to teach them something that most of them don't care about learning. Hah! They'd walk off.

Kids cannot walk off, of course, but their minds are equally flighty. So how to pull them into the lesson and keep them going? There are two ways a teacher can make that happen.

The first way is to have every child work on the same assignment, which begins so simply that even students who are unsure about more advanced work can do it easily. That way, every student has a chance to experience immediate success in class. Naturally the assignment then gets more complicated with each question, so the class can proceed at various paces, according to their skill level. Each kid should be engaged and move along according to his or her competence.

Then, whenever students come to a problem they can't solve, the teacher can work directly with only those particular students. In other words, only with those learners who are *stumped*, while the rest of the class surges ahead.

During the process the teacher may want to check for understanding with every member of the class. This is quickly done by asking the students to raise their hands *if they understand,* and then focusing on those students who are having problems.

A second way is for the teacher to immediately start circulating around the room, checking the efforts of *every student.* Some will have difficulty at certain points of the assignment. If the teacher gives a hint or solution and makes corrective comments out loud, the whole class can tune in and benefit. Thus every student can keep up with the progress made by the individual learners. Every child can learn to leap over the learning hurdles.

As a result, as the students continue to work their way "up the ladder," starting with the easiest items and advancing to the most complex problems, the teacher, still circulating, urges each child along. Yet even while monitoring the work of a kid in the back, the teacher has to speak to the whole room, thus showing Ebonie in the front row how to solve problem number 5.

So here's the choice: Does the teacher concentrate on the slower kids only or become a walking-talking teaching machine, hustling every child along?

Most often a combination of both approaches is used to ensure that every student gets some individual attention. As a consequence, little time is wasted, which is most important. And it means that even with today's shortened attention spans, every student—no matter what the achievement level—is on task, instructed, and inspired to reach his or her potential.

QUICK TEACHER QUIZ

Now let's pause, as the teacher probably would like to do at this moment in class. The teacher has to go on checking on all the kids, hour after hour. You have the luxury to stop and find out how your child's teacher measures up in this most difficult teaching strength.

Again, you can only assess this strength while observing a class. So make an appointment with your child's teacher. Once you're sitting in the classroom and the lesson has truly begun, get ready.

YES

___   26. Does the teacher get all kids on task quickly, within five minutes after the bell?

___   27. Is every student's work checked and every student called on at least once during class?

___   28. Are all students learning something and encouraged to try their best?

___   29. Does the teacher constantly monitor the class, ensuring a high time-on-task atmosphere for all students?

___   30. Are there follow-up or extra activities for those who finish quickly?

DOES YOUR CHILD'S TEACHER MAKE THE GRADE ?

Exceptions exist in teaching more than in other areas, but three or four YES checks are a good starting point. If you have trouble coming up with any YES answers, or if you're unsure about some of the questions, you can always call or e-mail your child's teacher. Your best approach, however, would be to ask the teacher about them at the next parent-teacher conference. There may be many reasons why several kids in class didn't make progress.

Therefore, forget about anything negative you observe and zoom in on the signs of excellence in this teacher. Forge ahead and just open the door to a meaningful discussion about teaching. In that way, the quiz questions will be a vehicle for school success, and that's the goal.

While you're thinking about those questions, search your mind and see if can't come up with more ideas about staying on task. If so, use the blank lines that follow to write down your thoughts.

_____

_____

_____

_____

_____

_____

Now let's apply what you learned about this tough teaching strength. Only then can your kids make real headway.

BRAIN GAINERS FOR YOUR CHILD

- Encourage Ebonie not to be bored in class. Tell her to keep listening to the teacher and concentrating hard.

- Give her your own best strategies for concentrating during a long lecture. Just say, "Look, this is how I fight the boredom blahs."

- Teach her how to ask pertinent questions about any school subject. Sit down with her one evening and write out a few practice questions for her to use next day.

- Ask her to give you a rundown of her favorite class every evening during dinner. Just the key points, please.

- Teach her to work through a work sheet on her own. She should do what she can first, while underlining the phrases or words that give her trouble. Later she can go back and attack the more difficult items.

ON A ROLL

- Tell Errick that reading a book is like having a private tutor, except that the private tutor is Errick himself. So he should ask himself, What's the lesson of this book?

- At dinner, ask Errick if he has any questions about his schoolwork, then discuss possible answers with him. I bet you'll learn something new right along with him.

- Introduce Errick to a professor at your local college. Just choose a free lecture together, attend it, and, at the end, ask Errick to ask a question out loud.

- Ask Errick to "own" his learning, to plan ahead for any free time he has in any class where he's ahead of the other students. He can get a textbook for the next level and start working independently.

- Tell Errick and Ebonie how proud you are of them for striving toward academic excellence every day. The way your kids are going now, they'll be sure to be A+ students before long, if they aren't already. And naturally that includes you as well.

HONOR ROLL

You want to make the honor roll too. You want to be the most supportive and teacher-empowering parent in your community. How can you do that? Easily.

As soon as your kids start bringing home improved grades, give credit where it's due. Then take out a sheet of paper and write a letter of commendation about your child's teacher. List three specific things this teacher has done to propel Ebonie toward reaching her potential.

Then make copies of the letter. Send one to the personnel director of your school system, another to the principal, and give the third copy to the teacher. No big deal—just put it in an envelope and place it on the desk.

Thank you for bringing out the best in Ebonie!

8 | Making Class Interesting

WHEW. But at least now the class is well under way, with every student immersed in work. That takes us another major task: How do you to keep it going?

In your role as teacher, you know that if your students lose interest, they're going to be bored. And bored students spell trouble. The fact that they don't learn what they're supposed to is the least worrisome thing. In fact, students just sitting quietly in their desks is your best scenario. Not so good is note writing, doodling, or reading comics or that hot teen 'zine. Worst of all is when they put the energy that should go into academics into acting up. That can range from flying paper airplanes to frustrating their fellow students to getting into fistfights.

To keep them busy and productive must be the teacher's goal here. But keeping them busy will only work if the material is presented interestingly. And that's easier said than done.

Definition In the classroom, *to interest* means to arouse, absorb, and hold the attention of every student in the class. While it's simple to interest a small studious bunch, to have all the kids eating out of the hand of the teacher, so to speak, is a tremendous job.

Most important is for the teacher to know the subject well and be able to add interesting tidbits, anecdotes, or related information. Kids learn best from examples that relate to their own lives and interests.

For that reason, sentences written on the board or on work sheets should reflect what's going on around the students. They should include names of people in the sports or entertainment

field that kids routinely discuss. Kids listen better to lectures if teachers sprinkle in school events, such as the prom, the result of the band competition, even what's for lunch in the cafeteria. Teachers must be energetic and yet have their instructional talks issue forth like a pleasant and gentle spring rain—without a struggle.

Details   Presented that way, the process of offering a lively hour of instruction seems easy when it really flows. But how hard it can be to make that happen!

The teacher has to have key questions prepared in advance and all related material, including the paragraphs to be read to the class, in mind. Teachers can't just take a ruler and point to items listed on the board. Kids expect more these days, and fortunately teachers now have much more in their instructional arsenals. They can trot out all sorts of fascinating learning tools, such as charts, cartoons, pictures, posters, newspaper clippings, maps, graphs, and artifacts—maybe even a paper or poem or ballad they wrote about the Vietnam War, with a guitar accompaniment. Whatever it takes to get kids absorbed in the lesson.

The teacher who gets fully warmed up to a subject may pull out puppets or pottery shards from the Civil War. Tapes and video clips help too, as do flash cards, color-coded cards, and various body movements, such as thumbs up or down, or clapping or even cheering. They may hand out gold stars, on occasion, to keep kids engaged. Tying in the lesson with what's new on the Internet, in music, or in age-appropriate movies can also be helpful.

Fact is, today's students require more active lessons than those of the past.

Actually, it's the genuine interest the teacher has in each student that keeps kids learning. Add to that the constant verbal interaction the teacher has with them, which should offer kids a variety of ways to answer, from responding themselves to calling on a classmate to reply for them. The main thing is not to over-look a single student: Leave no child behind! As a result, every student will feel that he or she is an important part of the class and doesn't dare slack off.

Half the hour is over, but the tempo must not slow. By using a multitude of top techniques, the teacher moves the instructional program along at a gallop, keeping the students on their toes during the whole lesson. Then at the end, ever the maestro, the teacher sums up what was learned:

- stating the new skills acquired, or
- listing them on the board, or
- holding up a folded poster, asking the kids to name the highlights of the lesson, and then unfolding the poster and pointing out if they were correct and what they might have missed.

Every lesson needs to be charged with energy and organized so that all kids participate to the best of their abilities. That task—to maintain the students' interest level on *high*—is a real challenge, but quality teaching demands it.

QUICK TEACHER QUIZ

Let's see how your child's teacher handles this tough task. Again, you can only observe this strength while present during a lesson. But you don't have to be there the whole hour. If your time is limited—join the club—choose a short period toward the end of class. Plan on five or ten minutes of observation, if you can, but remember: The end of a lesson will tell you a lot more than the beginning.

Again, please make an appointment with the teacher well in advance and explain that you want to come in during a class. Promise that you will be as unobtrusive as you can, and please be exactly that. Take your seat quietly wherever the teacher indicates, concentrate on the lesson while keeping an eye on all the kids—not just yours—and then check YES for success!

YES

____ 31. Does the lesson excite all the children and pull them in?

____ 32. Does the teacher know the subject well and use audiovisuals, including posters, tapes, and other materials, to add oomph to the lesson?

____ 33. Does the teacher teach briskly, accelerating student progress sometimes yet reteaching other times?

____ 34. Does the lesson touch on the kids' lives and interests, stimulate their curiosity, widen their horizons, and include various opportunities to respond?

____ 35. Are the middle and end of the lesson engaging, and does the teacher sum up what has been taught?

DOES YOUR CHILD'S TEACHER MAKE THE GRADE?

Count on three or four checks as being a good starting point on this section of the Quick Teacher Quiz. But if you have trouble coming up with any YES answers, or if you're unsure about some of the questions, you can always call or e-mail your child's teacher or just ask about them at the next parent-teacher conference. There may be many reasons why you can't put a check on some blanks. So rather than focus on what you don't notice, why not zoom in on the obvious signs of excellence? Then use the blanks as a springboard for a good talk with the teacher. In that way, the list will be a vehicle for school success.

And while you're thinking about the questions, take a moment and ask yourself: Do you have more thoughts about making class interesting? If so, use the blank lines that follow to write down any ideas you have.

_____

_____

_____

_____

_____

_____

_____

_____

BRAIN GAINERS
FOR YOUR CHILD

- Whenever you and Ebonie have a talk, ask her afterward what she learned from it. Say, "Tell me in a few words what I just discussed with you."

- Teach Ebonie how to make even a dull subject exciting by forcing herself to write down at least ten words or ideas during a lecture.

- Help her to grade herself each evening on how well she paid attention during the *whole* class time.

- Have her listen to an appropriate talk show on TV for ten minutes, and then have her summarize the main points.

- Teach her to predict what the teacher will talk about next, jot it down, and then see if she is right.

ON A ROLL

- Discuss with Errick how every topic can be related to our lives today and then ask him to relate the Middle Ages, for instance, to what's happening now.
- Ask him to totally flabbergast you every evening by weaving an unusual "big" word into the conversation at the dinner table.
- One day soon, take him with you to a class at the closest law school, after getting permission from that school's office to audit a class.
- Get him started taking class notes on his personal computer if that's workable at his grade level.
- Have Errick show his leadership in class and by his example teach his classmates that there's nothing cooler than concentrating in class.

HONOR ROLL

Soon Ebonie and Errick both will bring home the best grades ever. Way to go. You want to make the honor roll too, as the most supportive and teacher-empowering parent in your community. How can you do that? Simple.

Halfway through the grading period, most teachers give their students an interim report. Why don't you do the same? Except your interim report is just a little pat on the back for your child's teacher and colleagues. Buy a bag of peppermints. Put them into a bowl and place it in the teachers' lounge with a note: This is *mint* for you!

9 | Active Opportunities

WHILE CHAPTER 8 FOCUSED on the teacher's skill in relating relevant materials and presenting lessons in a lively manner with audiovisuals or body movements, this chapter deals with an even more amazing skill: that of giving every student a truly *active* role in the class and letting them take on more and more the role of partners in learning. In this case, being a partner refers to being engaged not only mentally but physically as well.

Definition   In the learning process, being *active* refers to being in action and moving around. That includes not only raising hands, nodding, and laughing but also getting up from the desk and walking around the classroom. Sounds like an invitation to sheer chaos, doesn't it? Just think, the teacher's twenty-five kids are all up and wandering around at will.

Of course, that's where quality teaching comes in. The kids do not move at *their* will but at the teacher's beck and call. And that is yet another major strength of the teacher: an amazing ability to shift one or two kids, or small or large groups of students around the room as if they were pieces on a chessboard. What an achievement for the instructor to do that with flair!

You see, it's one achievement to be a great actor—and all teachers need a dramatic air, a stage presence, and the ability to speak English well and correctly—but it's another achievement to invite all students to come onto the stage too when it will help them learn. But that's what teachers want: to involve all the kids mentally and physically and make them feel and act like stars in every class. So let's zoom in on this super-skill that teachers exhibit when they move from being the lead actor to being the class director. After all, the students are key, and how well a teacher can give each of them an active part in class is the question here.

Details   How in the world is that done? By hard work, preparation, and expertise. First, teachers must have a variety of teaching methods up their sleeves; then they must use them with competence. Therefore, they will include lively teacher-led instruction and break their lessons up into short segments with frequent pauses to assess for understanding. They will also schedule practice and repetition sections, and avoid any routine, monotonous, and unnecessary busywork.

We learn by doing! That's always been true and still is. So the more each student gets a chance not only to listen to new information but also to digest it, act on it, and include it with other knowledge, the more the student can achieve in the long run.

Teachers know this. That's why they vary their instructional presentations while always speaking correctly and using proper grammar. In other words, they use their superior verbal skills and their creativity to constantly change the pace and the "happenings."

One day the major part of the lesson is whole-class. The teacher lectures and the students listen and take notes. This is valuable in teaching new information.

The next day, the teacher demonstrates how to solve a problem on the board and calls on students to do the same. Getting up and working at the board involves the kids' bodies as well as their brains, which is important.

Later the teacher may split the class into groups of, say, four and has them sign up on a chart if they need help. Meanwhile the teacher makes sure that at least one student in each group can lead the activity. This give students a chance to move their desks, walk to the chart, and work with others—all activities that require real participation by everyone in class.

On yet another day, the teacher can use a series of questions to check for understanding. The class is divided into teams of two, which brainstorm for more questions on the topic. Then, the teams play a classroom-adapted form of *Jeopardy!* or Review Football, a game in which some questions count as much as a touchdown; others as much as a field goal. The teams of students vie for points as they dash to the board to write down their answers.

On still another day, student discussion is the major part of class. The teacher hands students tags as they enter the room. Each tag lists the bearer as an expert in a certain segment of what's been studied. Then the experts present small-group talks to their classmates. Or a panel of experts is assembled at the front of the room to debate two sides of a topic. Other times, advanced students can become "student teachers" for the day and teach the class.

Finally, one part of a lesson can be used for recitation: that is, a question-and-answer series during which the teacher asks the questions and accepts or channels or adds to the students' replies. Even better, students themselves can step to the front of the room and query one another.

No matter how the teacher decides to present this active instruction, all students need to participate equally. And that's only half the task. The other half is that the efforts of all students must be checked every day and not just the work of the two or three kids who always have their hands up. But what a great opportunity to rope in even the quietest and shyest youngsters. Masterful teachers do this by

- shuffling cards with the students names on them, or
- with the grade book in hand or by having a student keep score on the board, or

- with whole group responses alternating with row responses, or
- by going from one two-student team to the next one.

Only by calling on all kids in some way can the teacher get an accurate impression of what the class knows. Fact is, the best lesson is wasted if it's not understood and processed by the students. They must be truly active, not passive, and only frequent checking on their involvement can ensure that. Teachers need to know every day how well their students are doing.

Personal Note   Only when active opportunities are given in the classroom can students get really wrapped up in their learning. That lesson was starkly brought home to me after the Berlin Wall came down.

Born in Magdeburg, East Germany, a city near Berlin, I had for years wanted to visit the city of my birth. But there was a problem. Once the Iron Curtain was in place, Magdeburg was off limits. Even though I tried repeatedly to get special permission, I was never successful.

For example, in 1985 I made a special trip to Hannover, Germany, and from there to the small border town of Helmstedt, which was in West Germany then and the last stop before entering East Germany. Again I tried my best to get a visa to visit my birthplace, and again I was denied. So I simply spent a couple of days exploring Helmstedt, which looked deserted, almost a ghost town.

The train station was especially spooky. It was here that hundreds of Sri Lankan refugees tried to enter the West illegally only to be caught every time by British and German soldiers who shipped them back to East Germany in sealed trains. Since the Sri Lankan refugees had sold all their possessions and homes to get this far in their quest for freedom, they didn't want to get back behind the Wall. Many were so desperate that they attempted suicide, figuring a few days in a Western hospital would buy them time.

Fortunately four years later, this grim East–West German border atmosphere changed entirely. It was now a time for rejoicing. The Wall was gone! And on my next visit I was an official visitor *invited* to Magdeburg. By then it was 1991, and my dream came true. I would finally see the city of my birth, plus be among the first Western teachers to be a guest instructor in a formerly Communist school. What a thrill it was for me to present myself to my East German students that first morning. It was a huge class: forty junior high kids who all sat meekly in rows and looked at me silently.

Naturally I was prepared for them. I taught the assigned lesson in English and German, tried to draw the kids out by asking them questions, and so on, but while the students were respectful, they remained passive. They just looked at me and didn't say a word.

That went on for ten minutes as I frantically wracked my brain about how to involve this class of silent students. Soon I gave up on the suggested lesson plan and started talking about my experiences and my family. I even handed photos around. Still, it was eerily quiet in the room until one hand went up.

"But—do you know Mickel Jordann?" a boy asked, in heavily accented English.

"Sure," I said with a smile, and wrote Michael Jordan's name on the board. "We went to the same university, UNC–Chapel Hill," I explained.

From that moment on, the forty kids couldn't ask enough questions. Soon I had them writing sentences on the board using Michael Jordan's name. They also composed paragraphs in their notebooks, and later we had a discussion about what the students would do if they *were* Michael Jordan.

When the bell rang, the class didn't want to leave, and another group pushed in. Students shared desks, and some sat on the floor. With the director's permission, we kept the lively class going until lunchtime.

This was truly active teaching. *Whew!* I was exhausted at the end of the day but also beaming because every student had gained from my instruction. All eyes had sparkled. Next day was even better. The students came in the room, wanting to volunteer. They read their homework assignments out loud and were ready to proceed to the textbook. After all, Michael Jordan had gone to a U.S. college, and they wanted to be smart enough to attend a similar school someday.

On my last day as guest teacher, the students plied me with presents for my regular classes back at Orange High School in Hillsborough, North Carolina.

I accepted 150 individually wrapped chocolate candies, one for each of my students back home, and a gigantic candy bar for me, and flew back to North Carolina.

Off to school the very next morning, filled with the joy of teaching and, of course, bearing the generous gifts from East Germany, I looked at one of the candies closer before the first bell rang, and felt my face burn. It said in small print: CONTAINS 100-PROOF LIQUEUR!

Yikes. As my American students piled in, I quickly shared the huge chocolate bar with them. As for all that liquor candy, I turned it in to the office. And do you know what? For days afterward, whenever I walked in the office the whole staff, from the principal on down, smiled at me. They smiled at me *a lot!*

QUICK TEACHER QUIZ

Back to quality teaching. It must always include active opportunities for each student. Let's take a moment and see how your child's teacher measures up in this teaching strength. Again, you can only check on this if you're observing the class. So after making an appointment, please walk quietly into the room, sit in back, listen, and watch. Then it's simply a matter of recording what you see and hear. If you can answer YES, check below.

YES

_____   36. Does the teacher include instructional activities that allow students to move around during class?

_____   37. Does the teacher encourage all kids to participate actively in class by keeping score in a grade book, with a checklist, or on the board, while drawing out the quieter students and holding down the kids who always have their hand up?

_____   38. Is the teacher able to tell you on a daily basis about your child's work?

_____   39. Is the teacher's vocabulary appropriate, the grammar correct, and the voice quality good, and are the words pronounced correctly?

_____   40. Are students allowed to work in groups and make presentations, and are they encouraged to use proper English by example and reminders?

As in previous segments of the Quick Teacher Quiz, three or four YES checks are a good starting point. But there are exceptions. It may be that you visited the class during a "quiet" day, one on which the teacher scheduled instructional time for silent reading or essay writing. On such occasions you won't be able to watch the students move around a lot.

But most class days should include more than kids just sitting meekly in their desks with their eyes glued to a page. Kids are bundles of energy, and the master teacher both acknowledges that fact and makes use of it. So even on an ordinary day in school—actually there are no ordinary days because learning always entails so much excitement—an observer should see students up and about at least once during a lesson.

Look at the questions again, think about what you watched in your child's classroom, and count up your check marks.

You should find several, including those next to questions numbered 38 and 39.

But let's assume you have trouble coming up with any YES answers or are unsure about some of the questions. Once again just call or e-mail your child's teacher or, better yet, ask about them at the next parent-teacher conference. There may be a reason why on this particular day you couldn't observe the specific signs of quality teaching we talked about.

At any rate, don't panic. Rest assured that there is a reason for whatever you observed in class. So just concentrate on the signs of greatness in this teacher, then start a meaningful discussion. As a result, the list will be a vehicle for true school success.

And if thinking about these questions suggests extra thoughts and ideas about active participation in class, go ahead and write them down on the lines that follow.

_____

_____

_____

_____

_____

_____

BRAIN GAINERS
FOR YOUR CHILD

- Ask Ebonie to put together a weekly collage of what she learns. She can cut out pictures and words from magazines and glue them on a piece of construction paper that can be suspended from the ceiling in her room.

- When she invites her friends over, ask the children some questions and teach them how to take turns answering you.

- When having a conversation with Ebonie, correct her grammar and help her speak correctly.

- Help her think before she speaks by teaching her to wait a second or two, formulate her ideas, and then express them.

- Arrange a study-buddy date for Ebonie, so she and a few of her classmates can practice working in groups without getting sidetracked.

ON A ROLL

- Help Errick to spice up his oral presentation skills by teaching him to vary his sentence lengths.

- Instruct him on the use of gestures and direct eye contact when speaking.

- Ask him to catch you making a grammatical mistake. You'll pay him one dollar every time he catches you. Likewise he has to pay you a dollar every time you catch him. Naturally that doesn't include casual chitchat with his friends, but kids should know the difference between jawing and joshing with their pals and speaking more formally with their parents and teachers. Overall, please have a few laughs when Errick tries to sneak a "He be tripping" past you, then discuss what that phrase should be correctly—"He is tripping"—which then leads to the question, What does *tripping* mean?

- Make sure Errick knows how to present information with the help of charts, graphs, and videotapes. Let him practice with several computer software programs and help him script his camcorder chronicles.

- When Errick and his classmates do a group project, show him how to delegate specific assignments to other students, insist on everyone in the group doing a fair share, and "invite out" those members of the group who are slackers.

HONOR ROLL

Before you know it, you'll be having fun with reinforcing at home some of the same instructional techniques the teachers use at school. And soon your children will try their hardest to be on the honor roll, trust me. Of course, you will too.

For you, that means being the most supportive and teacher-empowering parent in your community. How can you do that? With a click of your computer mouse. Just type out the following words, then get creative with fancy fonts, cheerful colors, borders, and type sizes:

COUPON GOOD FOR
1 HOUR OF

_____

Then fill in the blank with one or two of the following ideas:

Tutoring a student in reading, filing papers, special clean-up time, researching extra materials, checking a simple test, counting absences and e-mailing parents of absent students, arranging a class party, making phone calls.

First, of course, ask the school principal what kind of "time coupon" is acceptable. Then go to it. In this case, you don't go *check-check-check*. Just go *click-click-click* with the mouse and print out those coupons, cut them out, sign your name to them, and send them to your child's teacher. And then congratulate yourself for being an active and creative education partner.

Think of what would happen if just one parent at every school in the country—in the world, even—would follow your lead. How many teachers would be inspired to work even harder because you, with your winning attitude, gave your best effort. Teachers, students, and parents working together form a circle. And you are making sure the circle is vibrant and powerful.

10 | Time to Evaluate

As YOU CAN SEE, a strong instructional presentation and superior content knowledge are interwoven. One depends on the other to manifest itself. Therefore, this teaching strength can appear in various forms in today's classrooms.

For that reason I want you to know the next three outstanding teachers. All you have to do is read on.

You will notice that again I introduce them to you under the headings of a good teacher, a better teacher, and the best teacher, but after you have met them, I'll ask, Do you agree with my evaluation? You might, or you might not. In any case, get ready to make up your mind, because here they come.

GOOD TEACHER Tyler Kim was born in Arizona to immigrant parents who insisted that their daughter excel in school and get a scholarship to college. While they didn't expect their daughter to go into teaching—in fact, they were hoping she would go into medicine—they were nonetheless pleased when Tyler decided otherwise.

"As long as she is happy," her mother said, and her father just smiled.

That's all it took to get Tyler even more fired up than she was already. She knew from her own experience how important it was to have good teachers. Remembering how she felt in first grade as she looked at the huge classroom and saw all the kids swarming around, she was determined to be extra sensitive to her students' needs. Her plan was to make her room a warm and friendly place where everything was in order, where every child

would feel comfortable, and a sense of security would predomi-
nate at all times.

That's why Tyler scurried around school like crazy three
weeks before it opened to get all her materials together. She
requested enough regular textbooks, plus five more, and signed
her name inside the front cover above where her student's names
would go later. Come what may, she'd be ready to issue the
books on Day 1. The extra books would be for the late enrollees
who usually trickled in during the first week of school. She'd be
just as ready for them as she was for the rest of the class. For that
was Tyler's special strength, anticipating her kids' needs. They
enjoyed having a teacher who was on the ball, which she was in
the smallest of details.

Before class started she always stepped behind the partition
in the back of her room where she had hung a small mirror and
kept a brush. Her glossy long hair was easy to manage but a
quick check and a once-over with the brush never hurt. As she
did this, she always rehearsed her opening statements for the
day. Of course, the day's lesson was posted, and the objectives
winked from the board.

But even more important was how Tyler got each student
involved from the moment the bell rang and kept them on task.
She told her students a continuous story about some kids traveling to another planet, then based the day's lesson on the problems the kids encountered. Her talent for storytelling was so
strong the students couldn't wait for her to get to the next segment, and as she did they hung on her words. Before they knew
it, Tyler had them doing their classwork as if they were on that
other planet too.

Making her students part of her story gave Tyler plenty of
chances to involve them in solving all kinds of problems and
using them in their own lives. She assigned them to various

groups and committees, set up deadlines that encouraged the kids to produce their projects quickly and yet accurately, and then motivated them to move ahead.

All her students felt a tremendous sense of achievement when they left her room, and yet learning seemed more like play. The students were never bored because they did bookwork interspersed with hands-on projects.

"Wonder what we'll be doing in Ms. Kim's room tomorrow?" they asked one another other over the phone most evenings.

Tyler knew it would be another exciting adventure.

BETTER TEACHER Mrs. Betty Lake can trace her ancestry in the United States back 200 years. Her forefathers came from Ireland, and she's been over there several times to visit. Even though she is a math teacher, she has never returned from her travels without something splendid for her classes. She knows that whatever polished chestnut or pebble she brings back with her, it always livens up the class. But there's little time wasted on stories and anecdotes, because from the moment the kids enter the room, they concentrate on the chunk of learning assigned for the day.

Betty, who has taught for almost thirty years, does share a few personal snippets from her life but nothing resembling science fiction. When she mentions her family, she tells how proud she was of her son, who was an outstanding student, and of her husband, who was a policeman. Both unfortunately are now gone. The son died in a motorcycle accident while in basic training. The husband died last year of lung cancer.

And yet Mrs. Lake is filled with optimism and hope. She looks at each student entering her room as if he or she were a younger version of her own child, or maybe the grandchild she never got to have. And so, in her serious but determined manner, she launches into the day's work.

Her work sheets and review sheets are always in a special spot, and students take turns handing them out. She doesn't ever have to appoint anyone. The kids just know automatically what to do. Also, it's Mrs. Lake's practice to begin with a quick overview of what was studied the day before, and as she takes the roll the students themselves volunteer to recap the previous lesson. They march to the front of the room and recite key points already learned.

By then roll has been taken so Mrs. Lake asks, What do you think we'll learn today?

Again, students volunteer all kinds of answers, and—well-instructed as they are—one by one they step over to the bulletin board and, on a piece of roller paper, jot down their predictions.

While the whole room is fueled with purpose, it's amazing how involved the students are, not only mentally but physically. But they move around the room with total respect for one another.

After everyone has had a chance to participate, Betty incorporates the various predictions listed on the paper into her opening remarks to the class. So in only a couple of minutes every student is on task and engaged because she personalizes the start of every hour of instruction. And that personal touch continues even throughout math class. Every work sheet has actual students' names listed. There is never any blah problem like, student A leaves his house on Main Street and walks to student B's house, which is three miles away.

No, her problems read like this: On Saturdays when Jeremy—a student in class—has finished watching cartoons on TV—here Mrs. Lake lists the real cartoon show Jeremy likes best—and decides to walk over to his friend Sam's house—Sam is Jeremy's best friend and is also in class—he takes a shortcut that saves 10 minutes. Keeping in mind that the walk usually would take 40 minutes, what percentage of time has he saved?

With real names and everyday situations in their math problems, the students can't wait to get their fingers on the work! They know how to pair off, or work in groups one day, in teams the next, and they try to do good work every day.

For when they do, Mrs. Lake smiles. And, hey, it takes a lot to get Mrs. Lake smiling.

She's usually stern and serious, but with a twinkle in her eye. She wears suits that have been updated and silk blouses that change slightly over the years, while her body type, resembling an apple, never changes. That's good because the community relies on her steadfastness.

She has so much teaching experience and that extraordinary teacher's stare that gets even a rambunctious kid in the back of the room quickly started on one of her many energy-consuming tasks. Plus she taught many of the students' parents and truly knows how to promote student achievement.

Her best friend is Mrs. Sanford, another long-time teacher.

BEST TEACHER Mrs. Glenora Sanford is the same age as Mrs. Lake and has taught just about as long, but that's where the similarities end. No nononsense business suits for Glenora. Although she weighs about as much as Mrs. Lake, she wears flowing long skirts and matching tunics and head gear from around the world. She's traveled around the globe, and from every capital she visited she brought back a hat, turban, or scarf.

With her dark eyes, beautiful dark skin, and unlined face, she often looks like a young girl as she shows off her hat collection—all intended to bring the world to her students. They don't even wait for the bell to ring. As soon as they get to school, they stick their heads into her room and check out what might be in store for them that day.

Too bad Mrs. Sanford keeps the chalkboard covered and doesn't reveal it until each student is seated. For that purpose she's had a world map mounted to the ceiling in front of the board that she pulls down.

So kids never know what to expect in Mrs. Sanford's room. She teaches French and speaks it beautifully. Naturally she greets the students in that language. Often she has a puzzle waiting on each desk that uses the irregular French verb forms for the day, and she tells the class that whoever finishes first can get another from the stack of supplementary materials she has.

Mrs. Sanford has copies of lessons from schools from the various countries she has visited. She uses them interspersed with her own work, then lets the students hear taped recordings from someone their age in Paris.

Other times the students write and design French greeting cards, video-conference with a college French class, translate French cartoons into English and vice versa.

At the end of the hour, the students linger and don't want to leave the room. When they are sick, they drag in anyway—for just Mrs. Sanford's class. By the end of the year, all her students have gained two or more years of French instead of the usual one.

Later, many students go on to major in French in college. Even if they don't, they never forget Glenora Sanford.

How could they?

YOUR CALL

Have you come to a decision yet? Have you made up your mind which of the three women you just met is the best teacher? Tough, isn't it, to decide? All three are outstanding educators. But just for a moment, pretend you're a judge instructed to determine which of the three teachers should receive a special award. Who has your votes for good, better, and best teacher? My answer comes at the end of the book.

TEACHER OF THE YEAR

Remember the Teacher of the Year (TOY) you met earlier and how impressed you were? Go back to the end of Part I and refresh your mind. What exactly was it you wrote down that made you really take notice?

Well, it's time for another meeting with the TOY at your child's school. Or maybe this time you want to go to another school in the district and meet their TOY or perhaps the other TOY nominees. Please don't shy away from visiting a school that's not your child's school. Remember, all public schools are your schools. You're an education reporter scouting out what makes great teachers tick. You're on a quest for quality teaching. So meet another top educator, or one from a previous year at your school. Then ask that special teacher just one question: *How do you get your kids to start learning from the moment they walk into your room and keep them continuously on task?* Write down the answer below:

Answer:_____

Now call that information to the attention of all teachers at your child's school. Start a column in the PTA newsletter called "Tips from our TOY." Or post it on the teacher bulletin board. Or on the school website.

Just think of what would happen if by your actions and encouragement every student in your child's school were to save two minutes of wasted time for every lesson or hour of instruction and turn them into learning time. Let's assume there are six school hours, which means a twelve-minute savings per day per kid. Then keep in mind the approximately 180 days most kids go to school. That means we have now saved 2,160 minutes saved per student, which adds up to 36 hours. Now let's take into consideration the fact that there are 800 kids enrolled in the average school. So you're saving 28,800 hours of academic learning time per year for just one school!

Imagine what would happen if that were to occur in every school. How much smarter all our kids could get. And all that because of *you*.

Part III: During the Lesson, Part 2

THIRD
STRENGTH | Student Management

*Disciplinary problems become opportunities for conveying values,
providing insights, and strengthening self-esteem.*

—HAIM GINOTT

IT'S REPORT-CARD DAY at the home of the Martinez family, who may live in your neighborhood. Theirs is the small but neat house with the yard with all those beautiful flowers. But let's not spend time outside. Let's go in and meet them: Mr. and Mrs. Martinez and their kids, Juan Carlos, who is in elementary school, and Juanita, who has just started high school.

This is the day they have both been waiting for. Juanita has been studying hard. She takes her schoolwork seriously. A pretty ninth-grader with a lovely face, a long dark-brown ponytail that swishes as she walks, and always freshly washed jeans and tucked-in tops that fit, she already has her future all mapped out.

She'd like to be a model someday, but that may not happen since she's only five feet five and may not end up being six feet tall, which someone told her is the preferred height for models. Plus, Juanita isn't that skinny either, compared to the models she sees in the teen magazines, though she's the right weight on the charts.

Anyway, becoming a model is just something she discusses with her girlfriends. She really doesn't want to be a model. What Juanita really wants is to go to college and get a degree in pharmacy. Actually, if it's possible, she wants to get a doctorate so she can teach in pharmacy school at the picturesque, ivy-covered old university that's sitting smack-dab in the heart of her state.

Wow—what great plans! She knows it won't be easy, yet she's determined. She knows high school is when grades start to really matter; in only four years, her transcript will be crucial. The university admissions office will get a copy of it, and Juanita wants it to be impressive.

Thoughts like these occupy Juanita's mind as she leaves for school this morning. "Hurry up!" she yells down the hall as she heads out the door on her way to where the bus stops. But as usual, her little brother, tall and in sixth grade, is dragging his feet.

Juan Carlos. That boy. Tell him one thing, and a second later he's forgotten it and you have to tell him again. But with Juanita's help he's recently been taking his schoolwork more seriously, especially since she explained to him that those sports superstars he so admires all have university degrees. So forget about football, basketball, and baseball, at least for an hour or two every afternoon, and hit the books. Fortunately, Juan Carlos has started to listen to his big sister. Lately he's been doing his homework.

That afternoon Juanita strides triumphantly into the house and calls, "Mama, Mama!" Mr. Martinez is in sales and comes home only on weekends, but his wife works as a dispatcher with the police department and has Wednesday afternoons off.

Now she emerges from the tiny laundry room. "Yes? Who's hurt?"

"Nobody, Mama. Look!" Juanita holds up her report card like a tennis trophy and then lowers it for her mother to read.

"Oh, that's great," Mrs. Martinez says as she reads over the various sections. "A . . . A . . . A . . . you made all A's! I'm so proud of you!"

Juanita beams, then says, a little subdued, "But I only made an A-minus in science, Mama, and that's supposed to be my best subject."

Her mother gives her a big hug. "Bet you can bring that up, if you want to. Isn't A-minus a 93 or 94?"

"That's right, Mama."

"Then all you need is a few more points next time," her mother says. She glances out the window into the backyard where Juan Carlos is slumping on a swing, his sneakers—his best pair!—scuffing and kicking against the dirt. "That poor boy! He looks so disappointed. Guess his school doesn't issue report cards until tomorrow."

Mrs. Martinez goes outside. "It'll be all right," she says to her son, after greeting him.

Juan Carlos turns abruptly. His face is dirt-streaked, as if he's been rubbing it. "No, it won't!" he yells. "Never ever. I'm just dumb. No good."

"What happened?"

"I don't know!" he yells. "Anyway, discipline isn't even a subject!"

After much prodding he finally hands her a wadded piece of heavy-stock paper. It turns out to be his report card and has nothing but Ds on it. "And after all the work I did!" he yells, She sees fresh tears standing in his eyes, which he hastily swipes away.

But Juan Carlos is right. Discipline isn't a subject, and yet under each of his low grades there is this teacher comment: *Needs to show more discipline.*

Juanita has joined them. "Maybe they made a mistake," she says. "One time my teacher marked me absent when I was just late. Mama, why don't you go to school and check on it? This evening is conference time."

Thirty minutes later, Mrs. Martinez is sitting across the desk from one of Juan Carlos's teachers. The boy came along but is skulking in the hallway. The teacher opens her grade book. "Look at that row of zeroes on every one of his chapter work sheets."

At that point, Juan Carlos, who's been listening, bursts into the room. "Man, I did that work," he protests. "See?" He opens his notebook and pulls out a stack of completed pages.

"Sorry, but I never saw any of them," the teacher says. "All completed classwork must go in my IN box." Turning back to her grade book, the teacher continues calmly, "And these zeroes are your homework grades."

"But I turned in all my homework!"

"Excuse me, but not at the beginning of class when it's due," the teacher says, indicating the rules posted on the bulletin board. She focuses her attention on Mrs. Martinez again. "What we have here is a bright student. But he must learn to get his mind off his classmates, pay attention to the rules, and complete and hand in his assignments properly."

On the way home, Juan Carlos skips along, singing, "Yeah-yeah, I still got a chance! I thought I was dumb but I still got a chance!"

His teacher has told him to do an extra-credit report on his favorite pro athlete. "Just this once, I may go back and change your grade," she said. "Of course, that's assuming you're going to show some discipline from now on."

Luckily Juan Carlos's problem was solved, but there are tens of thousands of students who don't understand that just being capable of doing good work isn't the same as having the discipline to perform well and steadfastly throughout their whole school careers. In fact, one brilliant test score averaged in with many low or missing grades never produces a top grade. It's the daily hard work, the ongoing effort, and the attention to detail that enhance learning and produce a great scholastic record.

Rules in school exist to make this process easier. In the classrooms of today, they're especially crucial. All students have to do is go by them. And all teachers have to do is make sure they keep them.

11 | Rules Posted and Enforced

TODAY'S ACTIVE CLASSROOM requires discipline, no doubt about it. For a few moments, picture yourself as a teacher directing several groups working on class presentations. That's like a harried movie director directing several films at once. Can you imagine? While he's dashing to one set to help out with the script, another needs him desperately about a problem with the props. And at the same time the actors working on yet another scene have a disagreement only he can settle. What a madhouse that would be.

Definition   These days teaching demands some of that same flexibility, energy, and organizational skill that directing a dozen movies simultaneously would need. And what the director would need most of all is actors with discipline. The same is true for teachers today. They need students with discipline, because without it kids can't reach their true potential.

So teachers have a double challenge when they teach. They have to get the content of their lessons across, as we discussed in Part II, while simultaneously instilling their class with the principles of good conduct, which we will do in this chapter.

To have a well-disciplined group of students means to have rules in place that are consistently enforced. School rules are simply directions for kids' behavior, and enforcing them is making sure that students abide by them.

Without rules that are enforced, little learning can take place. For example, once again picture yourself as a teacher. In your first-period class you have seven groups working simultaneously on various projects. Yet remember, your students are just kids; they're not necessarily the best collaborators. And they're cooped up in a small space—only one room, your classroom—with limited materials! So while they're all making progress, you, as teacher, have to dart back and forth to put out fires and inspire the various groups to surge ahead. That only works if you're tossing encouraging statements at one group, asking probing questions of another, handing a third group a supplementary book, referring the fourth group to the index of their text, applauding the fifth group on their speedy advancement, redirecting the sixth group to their purpose, and reteaching some basics to the last group.

The only way you could successfully pull that learning experience off is if—by your strong classroom management skills—you have rules and consequences in place that bring out the cooperation of your class. In other words, if you have taught the basics of classroom behavior and you (re)enforce them whenever needed. How is that handled? Carefully.

Details   From the moment the students walk into the room, the classroom rules have to be prominently posted (easy) and enforced (not so easy). Managing a class well depends on what types of activities you have in store. While it's not difficult to take care of student management during a whole-class lecture, it's more difficult in an active classroom where kids are in groups or moving from one learning station to another. In those cases the teacher has to be especially conscious of student conduct and ready for anything. What helps is to

- involve kids in the classroom management process,

- discuss the reasons for having discipline and rules, and

- ask kids to come up with some of their own rules and regulations (which may vary from activity to activity).

Besides the rules in your class, there have to be overall school rules that are broader than classroom rules and yet underpin and support excellent student conduct in school buildings and on school grounds. All the rules in the world, however, won't amount to anything unless the consequences of not following them are discussed, outlined, and posted as well.

Then comes the most difficult task. The teacher has to enforce the rules, administer the consequences, and, even more importantly, through the strength of teaching and personality and through practice and reminders, reemphasize the rules until they are deeply ingrained in every student. Only then will they automatically do the right thing, inside the classroom and out.

QUICK TEACHER QUIZ

Let's take a look at how well your child's teacher measures up in the rules department. A quick survey of the classroom will help you answer most of the questions. Others can be answered when you walk down the hall during a class change, or just by asking your child about the rules at school. Then all you have to do is check the spaces next to the questions whenever you can answer YES.

YES

____   41. Are the classroom rules posted prominently?

____   42. Are the consequences posted prominently?

____   43. Do the kids follow the rules most of the time?

____   44. Are school rules observed outside the classroom?

____   45. Are the students allowed to suggest and vote on some of the rules themselves?

DOES YOUR CHILD'S TEACHER
MAKE THE GRADE ?

Now go back and count how many YES checks you put on this segment of the Quick Teacher Quiz. Did you come up with three or four? That's good, if they include numbers 41 and 43.

Ideally, of course, you'd like to end up with all five questions checked. But, as we've said before, exceptions exist. Schools are hives of real kids, not robots.

If you had trouble coming up with *any* YES answers, or if you're unsure about some of the questions, why not call or e-mail your child's teacher? Even better, ask your child's teacher about them at the next parent-teacher conference. There may be good reasons why you can't put a check on some of the blanks, so let's take this opportunity to concentrate on the signs of excellence in your child's teacher and begin a meaningful, productive, and enriching discussion. As a result, the checklist will fulfill its main purpose: to promote school success.

While you're thinking about the quiz questions, can you think of more questions about school rules? If so, please use the blank lines that follow to write down any thoughts and ideas you have.

_____

_____

_____

_____

_____

BRAIN GAINERS
FOR YOUR CHILD

- Have rules and consequences dealing with chores and behavior at home in place.

- Discuss with Juan Carlos what consequences will occur when schoolwork isn't done.

- Ask him what privileges he should lose when homework isn't done.

- Decide on how to deal with low test scores, and find out from the teacher what she suggests.

- Post the rules, carry them out, and change them frequently as Juan Carlos gets older.

ON A ROLL

- Have rules and consequences for older children like Juanita also. The rules should be reasonable and flexible.

- Follow rules yourself, in traffic and in daily interactions with others.

- Be the best role model you can be, by continuing to learn new skills yourself and by improving as a human being.

- Encourage Juanita not to cave in to negative peer pressure.

- Find a way to let her meet an older honor student who has overcome many obstacles and yet is pursuing her scholastic dreams.

HONOR ROLL

It's only natural that with your kids striving to do the very best they can to earn top grades, you want to make the honor roll too. In the case of a parent, that means being the most supportive and teacher-empowering parent in your community. So think about that nice teacher Juan Carlos has. She's giving him a another chance to bring up his average. Now it's time to do something special for her. What might that be?

How about having the teacher's car washed? Could a student group, or a group of PTA parents and their kids, volunteer to wash the teachers' cars one afternoon after school?

In many school systems, the car wash is one activity student clubs undertake to raise money. So you wouldn't have to do anything except suggest the idea. Then cover whatever it costs to wash the car of your child's teacher. That treat would make anyone feel better instantly. Who doesn't love a spick-and-span car?

12 | Keeping Discipline

THE REASON SO MANY STUDENTS and parents have questions or doubts about school discipline these days is that over the past few years the word has fallen out of favor. In its place, the term *classroom management* is now used. It refers more to positive strategies than to the strict training some people associate with the word *discipline.* No matter what term is used, a calm atmosphere and order have to prevail in the classroom. Behavior problems must be anticipated and dealt with immediately and effectively, and in a professional manner.

Definition   For a moment assume again you're a teacher and back in the classroom with seven groups of students deeply engaged in working on their various major projects. Suddenly trouble starts, first with one group, then another. Soon voices are raised, a cussword or two sails through the air, books are slammed, and paper is bunched up and tossed everywhere. Now what?

Not to worry. Your child's teacher can easily handle this kind of situation. For one thing, no good teacher will ever let things get so far. For another, teachers have many discipline tricks or, if you will, classroom management skills, up their sleeves. They know a good definition of discipline is *controlled behavior,* which means guided behavior. And that means behavior that is conducive to learning and studying in a maximized manner.

Details   What are the teacher's classroom management skills? Among them are an insistence on students' good conduct, and the ability to prevent problems. While teachers are aware that students can get noisy and off-track quickly, they are alert and acutely aware from the moment the bell rings. This acute awareness keeps them tuned in to every child in the classroom. They also know that small infractions are best corrected immediately, so they won't mushroom into big ones.

As a result, teachers make eye contact with those students who are likely to build paper airplanes when not on task, and direct them back to work with pointed stares or glances like darts. Or they hand these students a note before class, telling them to be specially on task this day.

Also, teachers use their outstanding "overlapping" ability—they can easily take care of two or three tasks at once. For example, such a teacher would work with one group while listening keenly for any out-of-order sounds from the rest of the room. At the same time the teacher gives one student a football time-out sign, or a cut-it-out sign (during which the fingers of one hand mimic the movements of a pair of scissors). The other hand gives a stop signal to yet another group that's about to get rowdy.

Additionally, teachers have eyes in the back of their heads, or act as if they do.

Plus, teachers know that boredom breeds the bugging-your-buddy syndrome, so they speed up the lesson by increasing the tempo and moving the learning process into third gear. Too much time in groups or too much moving around can also cause discipline snags.

When kids work in teams or groups, which they like, they tend to chat with one another too much and meander into out-of-school territory. They just happen to discuss a TV show or the latest hot song or cool outfit. Fortunately, however, teachers have ways of keeping all kids on in-school terrain. By constantly moving purposefully around the room and by focusing kids back on the key points of the lesson again and again, teachers keep the students learning and leaping forward, engaging even the sleepy-heads, the withdrawn youngsters, and the turned-off kids.

In addition, during a review, for example, teachers manage to keep all members of the class on the alert by coming up with creative new ways to encompass everyone. Students can't act up when they know their name will be called any second. Teachers also learn from their colleagues about the best discipline measures and pick up on the latest student management techniques. Thus, while their underlying rules of behavior stay the same, they have a constantly changing menu for dealing with school misbehaviors and preventing them. This includes getting kids focused on learning from the moment they step on the school grounds.

In classroom management—or discipline, if you prefer—prevention is more than half the battle.

QUICK TEACHER QUIZ

Let's see how your child's teacher measures up in this important teaching strength—the discipline keeping. You will have to observe a class to assess that strength, but it doesn't have to be for more than ten minutes. Even in a very short time you can get a feel for how well your child's teacher manages the students. All you have to do is be alert and watchful during a few minutes of class. Look around the room, observe the students, hear what they're saying, and see what happens should they wander off the learning path. And then it's easy. You simply pick up your pen and, if you can answer YES, check below.

YES

____   46. Does the teacher have all students under control and supervision?

____ 47. Are all students, even sleepy or disinterested ones, encouraged, involved, and motivated to participate?

____ 48. Are misbehaving students caught *before* they misbehave?

____ 49. Does the teacher circulate the room constantly, and stand by the door during class changes in order to supervise what's going on in the hall?

____ 50. Does the teacher know and use the latest discipline practices?

DOES YOUR CHILD'S TEACHER
MAKE THE GRADE?

While exceptions always exist, know that three or four checks are a good starting point. But if you had trouble coming up with *any* YES answers, or if you're unsure about some of the questions, call or e-mail your child's teacher. Or, better, ask about them at the next parent-teacher conference.

There may be lots of reasons why you can't check off some of the blanks. So rather than focus on anything negative, pay attention to the signs of excellence in this teacher before engaging in a meaningful discussion. In that way, you're fostering more school success.

By the way, while you're thinking about the questions, can you think of more about classroom management? If so, use the blank lines that follow to write down any thoughts and ideas you have.

_____

_____

_____

_____

BRAIN GAINERS FOR YOUR CHILD

- Insist on good behavior at home.

- Encourage Juan Carlos to always use his best manners.

- Tell him that from now on you will use some gesture, such as gently tugging on his sleeve, as a signal to stop him from saying a bad word or from acting obnoxious in public.

- Teach him to say *no* to anything you don't want him to do, no matter how many times his buddies try to persuade him.

- Make sure Juan Carlos has the opportunity to make friends who are studious and care about their grades.

ON A ROLL

- Ask Juanita to share her hints for staying out of trouble with her younger brother.

- When your kids do their homework, be close by, so you can keep an eye on their work, especially when they're on the Internet.

- Anticipate the temptations and negative influences Juanita will face as she gets older and plan how to deal with them.

- Make sure she is part of a faith-based group, so she can associate with kids who have similar uplifting interests.

- Get to know her school's guidance counselor and pick up pamphlets and other materials to help you raise youngsters who are disciplined and have a strong moral character.

HONOR ROLL

It's that strong moral character that will propel your kids to push themselves even farther in school and at home. You know how contagious a positive atmosphere is. So expect to be bitten by the bug to do still more to enhance your kids' education. In your case that means be the most supportive and teacher-empowering parent in your community.

Talk with your kids at least once a week about the importance of being on one's best behavior in school, and then ask them, Do you remember a teacher you had in the past who made sure you conducted yourself extra well and motivated you to follow the rules? Who was that teacher? And while Juanita and Juan Carlos are remembering, think back yourself to the teacher who first instilled discipline in you.

Then all three of you sit down and write personal thank-you notes to that man or woman whose special care helped make you a better student and a better human being.

13 | Dealing with Disruptions

"AMAZING TEACHERS!" you're saying now. "I never knew they had so much on their plates."

You're right, they do. They can never coast along and rest on their laurels. Teaching is a profession that never has a routine day. Teachers must always expect the unexpected and be poised and ready for many interruptions.

Oh, those interruptions. Many of them come over the intercom from the principal's office concerning changes in the bus schedules or some emergency information based on the weather. Or they notify students about the rescheduling of an athletic event, the sale of yearbooks, even the lunch menu in the school cafeteria. *Today the following delicious dishes will be served: Corn dog with green peas, tossed salad, fruit cocktail, cake squares with chocolate icing. . . .*

Definition Naturally most interruptions have an important purpose and can give students a quick breather, but for the teacher they usually serve only to upset the order of the lesson or break their students' concentration. Therefore teachers moan, "Just when my class was going so well, on comes a student rap about some ridiculous raffle."

There are nonintercom interruptions as well. They can come from the teachers' own devoted colleagues, since students have special needs and may be pulled out of class for a test by a speech pathologist, or a conference with a learning-disabled specialist, or a teacher working with the hearing or speech impaired, for instance.

They may also come from a hard-working assistant principal who is investigating who stopped up the boys' toilet; from a security officer sniffing out a possible report of drugs or weapons in a student's backpack; or from a guidance counselor, school social worker, or nurse whose job it is to help students with personal problems or health issues. No matter what the cause, these interruptions are endless and can eat into teaching time, thus frustrating the teacher.

Then, at the very moment the class has finally settled down again, the most frustrating things occur—the disruptions caused by students themselves, which can range from slightly annoying to absolutely maddening. There are the students who check in late because of a bus problem, or because they or their parents overslept, or because they had a dental or other appointment. Other students have to visit the rest rooms every hour, some of them legitimately. New students are enrolled and old students move to other towns or states, so the class membership tends to fluctuate.

The worst disruption could be the talking and cutting up in the classroom by students not yet on the same page of rules. But whatever the origin, teachers must be on top of things. They know that an unbroken day is unheard of. So early in the school year they instruct their students to continue working quietly unless directed otherwise, while the announcement box comes to life, while visitors pop in, and while classmates leave, return, or try to cause a mini ruckus. Or while one particularly dramatic student has a major meltdown.

Details   Fortunately, teachers plan ahead so that students surge forward, no matter what crops up in the room. Students follow established routines for going to the rest room and coming to school late or after an absence. The teacher has a hall pass system that kids follow; otherwise no more hall pass! Late arrivals know there's a folder for them in a specific place telling them what to do until the teacher can take the time to catch them up. And students returning to class after being absent know exactly where their makeup work is waiting for them, while new students have several files waiting for them that include diagnostic tests and basic introductory materials.

Plus the teacher always has a stack of stimulating alternate assignments for youngsters who for some reason or other are stuck, stymied, or stumped. Along with these alternate assignments, fun activities and puzzles are waiting for the student who's having a bad day, as well as notes written in advance for students who might freak out when a difficult concept comes up.

Fact is, some kids do better coming into the teacher's room at lunch or after school to be taught individually and without an audience. Furthermore, some notes can spell out the more serious consequences for continued student disruptions and can be given to a student upon entering the class. But usually all it takes is a personal memo from the teacher to the student that says: *Today remember to keep working until I say stop. I bet you can do it.*

After a few days with a personal reminder like this, most students won't need one anymore. Therefore, teachers don't dread disruptions. On the contrary, they welcome them as just another chance to develop super strategies for having the smoothest running class possible.

QUICK TEACHER QUIZ

How does your child's teacher measure up in this area? Naturally, you have to visit the class to be able to find out. If you have a choice, please go early in the morning or near to the end of the school day to check out how the teacher handles disruptions, since that's when most of them occur.

Then sit back in the seat you were given and wait—for the first announcement to come on, for one student needing the rest room, another asking to go to the library to renew a book, a third one being summoned to the office, and a fourth one having to sign out early because she's getting braces, and watch what the teacher does.

Oh, how unruffled, how prepared for all eventualities. And then you just smile, look at the blanks and hurriedly *check, check, check* if you can answer YES.

YES

____ 51. Does the teacher deal quickly and effectively with disruptions?

____ 52. Does the teacher hand out consequences to disruptive students and make sure they comply?

____ 53. Does the teacher keep the rest of the class working quietly while dealing with the disruptions?

____ 54. Does the teacher return to teaching smoothly, so the class continues to flow and no time is lost?

____ 55. Does the teacher stay calm at all times, having planned a response for whatever interruptions may occur?

DOES YOUR CHILD'S TEACHER **MAKE THE GRADE?**

While exceptions exist, know that three or four YES checks are great, especially if they include number 55.

But if you had trouble coming up with *any* YES answers, or if you're not sure about some of the questions, why not call or e-mail your child's teacher or, even better, ask about them at the next parent-teacher conference. There may be several reasons why you can't check some of the blanks. So rather than look for something negative, zero in on the signs of great teaching you've just seen and wait for an appropriate time to bring up what's bothering you.

While you're thinking about the quiz questions, you may think of more ideas about handling disruptions. If so, go ahead and write down any thoughts and ideas you have on the lines that follow.

_____

_____

_____

_____

_____

_____

_____

BRAIN GAINERS
FOR YOUR CHILD

- Make sure that Juan Carlos isn't sitting next to a troublemaker in class.

- Help him control his temper by teaching him to breathe deeply and count silently to ten or think of all the pro athletes he admires.

- Show him how to get back to his homework after he gets interrupted at home.

- Teach him to have patience at home and in school.

- Set up a system with his teacher so she'll let you know every week how well behaved Juan Carlos was. If he had a good week, give him a small reward.

ON A ROLL

- Buy Juanita a journal to write in when there's an interruption in school.

- Make sure she has lots of extra reading books. Try to get a copy of the reading requirements for the next grade level for her, so she has something else to do during the many disruptions that crop up during the school day.

- Teach her to take a break from prolonged study to get renewed energy.

- Insist on her getting some exercise, preferably with you. Can you two go for a walk three times a week?

- Show her how you lessen any stress and frustration that come as a result of constant interruptions. Then she can use her energy to study extra hard.

HONOR ROLL

Of course, you want to make the honor roll too. What can you do to be the most supportive teacher-empowering parent in your community? Check to see what de-stressing programs exist for your child's teacher. Is there a treadmill teachers can use? Can they walk around the track? Is there a coach who can mark off a one-mile segment on the walkways that meander around your child's school?

Teachers get extremely stressed out by the frequent announcements and interruptions during their lessons. While they realize how important those are, they need a way to lower their stress level. By insisting that the school do something about that, you're helping your child's teacher feel better and work under better conditions. Good for you!

14 | Achieving Best Behavior

OFTEN WHEN WE THINK OF STUDENT BEHAVIOR we shiver. That's because we have all observed examples of bad behavior in kids or watched it on TV, where it seemed funny. But in reality there's nothing funny about children who are rude to their teachers, who don't want to do their work, who fight and act out aggressively, and who are defiant to school authorities.

We worry that this inappropriate behavior will get only worse the older the kids get. And our worries are justified; wild kids, when unchecked, get only wilder, like a fire in the woods that gets out of control and soon consumes a huge area. In schools also, a climate of unruliness can spread and lead even the better behaved students astray. We have to have acceptable conduct, but *best behavior* is what we should strive for, especially in our schools.

Definition The behavior of students is the way in which they act in class. And *best behavior* is the finest conduct kids are capable of. To foster it, teachers need to stay calm, not overreact, and be confident that they can handle any problem they may encounter.

That starts with predicting bad behaviors. When teachers know from experience or through talking with their colleagues what might trigger unacceptable behavior in certain students, they can remove the triggers. That entails having a predictable classroom with consistent and reasonable rules and consequences.

Unlike scholastic instruction, which requires varied materials to infuse excitement into the learning process, getting kids to act right should be a strategy of consistency. What is wrong one day has to be wrong the next. Only in that way can kids find the security they need to be and act their best.

Details   Beyond having some reasonable rules and getting the kids to behave acceptably, the teacher should use additional tactics to get students to develop good conduct and character. Punishing a child for misbehavior is only half the task. The second half is teaching the youngster not to make the same mistake again and to become a role model for others. Therefore, all classrooms need to have such a good and uplifting climate that all students will not only learn the most but also become the best they can be.

It is important to teach kids not just to go by the rules but to go beyond them by being kind to each other, being helpful and encouraging, and rejoicing in their classmates' successes. In word and deed, the teacher can highlight the finest character traits that exist in the human race. Students can read about heroic, honest, and virtuous people and discuss them. Great role models can also be found in the heroes of the past as kids research the lives of leaders from around the world who made a difference then and now.

During a question-and-answer session, the teacher can then emphasize the positive qualities in the heroes students read about, and through warmth, acceptance, and high expectations toward even the less than perfect student help the class members to work together and maybe even undertake a special project outside school.

One way of getting a class to pull together is by dispensing praise and compliments freely. This establishes a positive tone. Recognizing any improvements a student makes and encouraging him or her to improve even more should always be part of the daily lesson plan.

Another way to turn a class into a cohesive team is for the teacher to take every opportunity to validate student comments and to extend their thinking even further, not just as far as social studies is concerned, for example, but also as far as society is concerned. Each positive act by a teacher, whether it's a smiley face drawn on a paper, a compliment for the whole class, or a special "celebration of success" when every child makes either A or B on a test has a major influence on the end results next time around.

By every means possible, the teacher should create a classroom atmosphere of heightened respectfulness and top performance. Bullying and teasing will fall by the wayside. Soon even the students will say only nice things about each other and cheer their class members on to more success.

QUICK TEACHER QUIZ

Let's take a minute to celebrate your success in learning about the major teacher strengths. Then examine how your child's teacher measures up.

I bet he or she does very well. And you'll be so pleased when you sit in on one of your child's classes—of course, only by permission received a week or two in advance—and absorb the positive atmosphere in the room. As you let that soak in, read the quiz questions and nod to yourself as you observe an abundance of positive signs. Then just check everywhere you can answer YES.

YES

____   56. Does the teacher praise all the kids in some way
              every day?

____   57. Does the teacher help students, especially if they
              were wrong, by trying to understand why they did
              what they did and then expect improvement?

____ 58. Does the teacher give supportive statements about any improvement, be it ever so slight?

____ 59. Does the teacher give feedback to students that encourages them to expand their thinking?

____ 60. Does the teacher validate all kids verbally or with a smile or nod or applause or positive note?

DOES YOUR CHILD'S TEACHER MAKE THE GRADE?

While there are exceptions, three or four checks are a good starting point.

But if you had trouble coming up with *any* YES answers, or if you're unsure about some of the questions, you can always call or e-mail your child's teacher. Maybe a better plan would be just to ask about them at the next parent-teacher conference. Many reasons exist for why you can't check off some of the blanks, so please don't get bogged down with anything negative. Instead, recognize the many signs of excellence in this teacher and then start a conversation to find out what you can do to help him or her become the best teacher possible. As a result, the checklist will be a handrail toward school success.

While you're thinking about these questions, does anything else come to mind? If so, please jot it down.

_____

_____

_____

_____

_____

_____

BRAIN GAINERS FOR YOUR CHILD

- Hug and praise your child every day for something.
- When checking over your child's homework, find a specific plus to mention and be proud of.
- Post at least one good report or homework paper on the fridge every week.
- Turn off the TV and allow your child to grow up without the constant barrage of bad news.
- Make sure to provide lots of great books and stories to read about people who have done heroic deeds and prevailed against all odds.

ON A ROLL

- Say positive things about the world, society, your neighbors, and yourself.
- Over the supper table, have hopeful and positive stories to share and teach Juanita not to be judgmental.
- Encourage her to tutor Juan Carlos or other younger kids in the neighborhood.
- Help her develop a healthy and high self-esteem by providing her with real role models and strong women leaders.
- See if she can't become a teacher's helper one day after school, or volunteer to do simple tasks in the school office or guidance department.

HONOR ROLL

That extra bit of effort Juanita makes to help out at school will reinforce her good feelings about herself and her capabilities. The more she gives to others, the more she gets in return. The same goes for you. You want to make more of a contribution to education yourself. That means you're aiming for the honor roll too, just like your kids. Only in your case, you're trying to be the most supportive and teacher-empowering parent in your community. How can you do that? Bag some bagels.

One dreary morning when the sun is hiding behind the clouds, bring sunshine to the teachers' lounge. (Naturally you'll want to get an OK from the principal first.) Show up with a bag of bagels, some cream cheese, plastic knives, and napkins.

Then just slice the bagels open, spread on the cream cheese, and watch for the smiles on the teachers' faces. That thoughtful gesture of yours will ripple through many a classroom, believe me.

15 | Time to Evaluate

ARE YOU READY TO MEET ANOTHER GROUP of outstanding teachers?

They're just like those your child has this year or will have: committed, caring, and competent. Again, they appear under the headings of a good teacher, a better teacher, and the best teacher. Yet in the end, that is a distinction only you can give them. You can agree or disagree with my evaluation, but only after you have met them and seen in person how they manage their classrooms. I bet you'll be impressed.

GOOD TEACHER Marco Rodriguez never planned to go to college, let alone become a teacher. From the time he could remember, all he ever wanted was just make it alive out of the tough neighborhood in which he lived. Fortunately, in junior high he was lucky enough to attract the attention of the wrestling coach.

Marco wasn't tall or heavy, and while he could outstare the toughest bullies, all he could do when they took a swing at him was run like the wind. But even a great runner can get cornered—which happened to Marco more than once. So after getting yet another black eye and broken nose, Marco started hanging around the gym after school. That's when the wrestling coach took him under his wing. And from then on, Marco started using his books seriously. "You can't be on the team if you don't have good grades," the coach said.

Soon Marco was making up missed work, in addition to not having to run anymore when the neighborhood bullies picked on him. In fact, he became good buddies with other boys his size and started a martial arts program while still in high school. That led to his renting space in a shopping center to teach Tae Kwon Do. The income from his classes paid his tuition at the local college, and then there was only the question of what to major in.

Business seemed an obvious choice. But the day Marco attended his first economics class and took the bus home, he ran across a bunch of school-age boys just hanging out during school hours. The older ones were all swagger and surrounded Marco, demanding his money. But the smallest boy looked pitiful and scared out of his wits.

"Sure, I'll give you what I got," Marco said with a chuckle, pretending to get out his billfold. Instead, he assumed one of his martial arts stances. The big guys scattered, but the scared kid tripped over his unlaced sneakers, so Marco grabbed him and walked him down the street to the middle school, where he was skipping. From then on Marco checked on that boy once a week, which led to his talking to the boy's whole class one afternoon.

Before long, Marco switched to education. This career hasn't provided him with the three-piece suits and fast cars he dreamed of, but now he has something better—a huge following of kids, an ever-growing fan club. Every student in school who gets in trouble by misbehaving becomes a member.

Often while Marco teaches, there are several older kids sitting in the back of the class, some by choice and others by the insistence of other teachers.

Marco is strict. He allows no deviation from the rules, and yet it's funny the way he can anticipate any little misdeed far in advance. Class is always exciting just from the standpoint of waiting to see what Mr. Rodriguez will say today to the kid who is late, who talks out of turn, or who doesn't raise his hand before blurting out an answer.

Some kids actually take it as a badge of honor to have been singled out for correction, and talk about modeling their lives after Mr. R, as they call him.

"Hey, if it weren't for R"—they drop the *Mr.* when out of his hearing range—"I'd be hanging with a gang."

"Yeah, man, me too."

BETTER TEACHER Chandra Halston started her college career as a member of Marco's economics class. Instead of quitting, however, she stuck with her business major, graduated with honors, and got her MBA. Was she triumphant!

Her grandfather, who once share-cropped in Alabama, couldn't read; her mother had only a high school education; and here she, Chandra Halston, was fulfilling her dreams!

As soon as she was hired by a megabank in Charlotte, North Carolina, and got her first hefty paycheck, she started to make herself over. She straightened her beautiful black hair, let it grow down to her shoulders, and gave it a soft under-flip every morning with the curling iron. Her skin was perfect already except for those darker patches under her eyes that had developed during college when she stayed up all night studying.

But never mind. A little concealer matched to her medium-brown skin tone took care of it, plus some shine on her lips. And voilà! In her business pants suits, brilliantly hued silk tops, and stacked heels, Chandra was ready to take on the world.

She loved her job. She knew she had caught the attention of the director and was on the fast track. What set her apart was that, being single, she thought nothing of working after hours, weekends, and holidays—until the day she met a co-worker.

DuBois Amons! He was tall and intense, reed-thin with a pencil mustache and small round glasses, and his education outstripped Chandra's. She had never before met a man with bigger dreams than hers. Except—shockingly—his had nothing to do with money. He was just working in banking to pay off his student loans, which he had accumulated by getting a law degree in addition to his business credentials. Then he was going to open up a nonprofit organization for underprivileged kids. From corporate greed to helping kids in need!

"How're you going to finance that?" Chandra asked him on their second date, which was quickly followed by a third. She wasn't going to let this special man get away, no sir.

"Oh, it won't cost much to start up my program," DuBois said. "It's going to focus on matching schools in poor neighborhoods with thriving businesses. What do you think?"

"About what?" Chandra said, trying to remember what they had been talking about. She was that struck with DuBois.

"Would you like to accompany me next week?" he asked. "I'm going to visit the kind of school I have in mind."

Chandra thought *fourth date!* and nodded.

When they got to the school, she couldn't believe her eyes. There were all these high school girls, many of them of color, milling around in the hallways during class time. They were loud, their clothes were totally inappropriate, their hair was a mess, and they looked plain lost. Several were pregnant and only in tenth grade!

"See why this school needs to get a boost from business?" DuBois asked Chandra as they dodged puddles and fallen plaster where rain had come in through the roof.

"You sneak," Chandra said. "I could just smack you."

"Pardon me?" DuBois stopped and looked at her over his glasses.

"Now I know why you really brought me here."

In a short time Chandra applied for a lateral-entry teaching position. That meant she didn't need a teaching certificate right away but would be given time to earn it during her summers.

That was two years ago. Since then she has taught quite a few of those girls who first drew her to teaching; boys too. What she gives them is what helped her along the way—rules to follow and the caring to make sure they do it. She has consequences for misbehavior and follows through. What helps most of all is telling the class her own story.

Often a student will say, "Excuse me, but that was, like, so dumb, you know. Man, giving it all up, you know. That big job and, like, the big income."

"But now I get to help you make it there," Chandra says, with a smile. "So in effect I'll do even better. Because someday when all of you are successful, it'll reflect back on me. You know, teaching is like a mirror. The better I make you look, the better you make me look."

"Ms. Halston, Ms. Halston, you're pretty already," her students say.

"Not as pretty as you will look and feel when you make that A on my economics exam tomorrow. Now, get your heads off your desks, sit up straight, and let's get started."

BEST TEACHER

When Jim Ennis was asked to coach the track team, he said, "Absolutely not." But when no one on the faculty volunteered, he agreed to give it a try. Why not? The extra duty paid a small supplement, which he'd use to buy his wife a present for their twenty-fifth wedding anniversary.

From then on, Jim Ennis was on the athletic field every afternoon with dozens of boys and girls, putting them through their routines.

What a switch that was! Jim looked like a modern Shakespeare with a balding head, hair long on the sides, and what his students called an "old-fashioned" face. They meant Mr. Ennis seemed to live in the past. He and his wife had built their own log cabin, huge but with few modern amenities. No TV, would you believe it? Just lots of books and marble pedestals on which the busts of famous English writers—like William Wordsworth, Lord Byron, and William Makepeace Thackeray—perched.

"William Makepeace Thackeray?" the student asked. "What kind of a name is that?" But it got them interested in the class on English literature that Jim taught, especially since he always dressed like the author they were reading at the moment.

It was not unusual to see him wear a cap and a flowing scarf or watch him drape a cape around his shoulders as he greeted his students. More unusual was to see him still wearing some of the same props at track practice. He was often so absorbed in his material that he forgot to take off the fake beard he had stuck on that morning or remove the ruffled white collar.

But Jim Ennis was never too busy to pay attention to his main job: running a great classroom. The student who stepped into Mr. Ennis's realm was immediately immersed in the poems of John Donne or whatever other great English writer was on the agenda for that day.

Jim even used expressions and phrases taken out of the works to be studied to post his rules and requirements. That was especially challenging when his classes studied Chaucer. Because Jim not only taught great literary selections but used them as springboards for his rules, kids had to hang on his every word not to miss anything. They came to class with a sign that said DO NOT DISTURB! and hung it outside his door. Then they tried to see who could behave the best. The room was so quiet they could hear the creak of Mr. Ennis's old shoes. All because Jim Ennis lives his work.

No one was surprised when the track team won the championship. Before the final meet, the coach jumped on a bench, velvet cape trailing, exhorted the team to give their utmost, and then screamed:

> *Blow, winds, and crack your cheeks! rage! blow!*
> *You cataracts and hurricanes, spout*
> *Till you have drenched our steeples!*
> —SHAKESPEARE, *KING LEAR*, III, ii, 1–3

YOUR CALL

Now that you have met all three outstanding teachers, which one do you think is best? Can't decide? Then just for a moment, pretend you're a judge and have to choose which one should receive a special award. Who has your vote for good, better, and best teacher? Wait for the answer until the book's final chapter.

TEACHER OF THE YEAR

Let your mind wander back to your own school days. Can you remember one or two teachers who still stand out in your mind after all these years? If so, then they're *your* Teachers of the Year (TOYs). Maybe you've already written them a thank-you note, but now is the time to track them down, pay them a visit, find out what their special quality is or was, and get their comments on how education is today.

Learn from those great teachers of the past and encourage other parents to do the same. Maybe one of your former teachers can give a talk to your PTA and provide some insight on how schools have changed. Also, most communities have chapters of the state and national retired teachers associations. Contact them and enlist their help. Teachers who taught for many years are fountains of wisdom. Tap into them now and share the knowledge.

Then, working in a partnership with teachers, be they beginners, mid-careerists, or retired ones, and with students, you're becoming the best parent you can be.

So let me be the first say, Good for you. You're truly an A+ parent.

Part IV: After the Lesson

FOURTH
STRENGTH | Testing

*I do not know anyone who has got to the top without hard work.
That's the recipe.*

—MARGARET THATCHER

It's a regular school night at the Lee home across town: nine-thirty, and things are beginning to wind down for the day. Mr. Lee has kicked off his shoes and put his feet up in the den, where he is slowly reading the paper that he only had time to skim that morning. Mrs. Lee is in the kitchen wiping counters, happy that everything's planned for tomorrow. The sandwiches for lunch are already wrapped and nestled in the fridge, right next to the freshly baked cake squares, whose aroma still lingers.

Young Lee, their son, a tall sixteen-year-old high school student, is hunkered down at the computer *click-click*ing away. He's researching what life was like in England between 1340 and 1400. Mr. Ennis, his English teacher, will hold forth on Geoffrey Chaucer's *The Canterbury Tales* tomorrow, and Young wants to be good and ready.

Where is Mimi, their eighth-grade daughter with the snapping eyes, cap of silky nut-brown hair, and ever-smiling face? She's in her room getting ready for bed, as she should by now.

But suddenly there is a scream from her, followed by another one, and then Mimi wails, "I can't do it!"

Mr. Lee is the first to arrive in the girl's room. "What's wrong?"

Mimi has stopped screaming. She's hunched sobbing over her desk, which is littered with stacks of notebooks, papers, and folders. "I . . . just . . . can't . . . *do* it!"

Her father is concerned. "What are you talking about?"

"This!" Mimi cries, sweeping her hand over the mess.

"Your homework?"

"Uh-uh. I got that done."

"Then what is it?" Mr. Lee is beginning to sound impatient.

"I have a—a big test tomorrow," Mimi sputters. "And I'm—I'm scared."

Mr. Lee pulls a chair over to his daughter's desk. "So what's on this test?"

Mimi wipes her eyes. "Everything that's on the third review sheet."

Quickly Mr. Lee starts flipping through the folders and notebooks but can't find it. "Have you lost the sheet?"

"No, she hasn't," Young says. He's just come in. "It's in her hand, Dad."

"OK, then." Mr. Lee extracts the wrinkled sheet from Mimi's wet fingers and scans it. "Do you know your definitions and all of chapter three?"

"Yes." Mimi sniffles.

"Let's just make sure, all right?"

In five minutes, Mr. Lee has asked Mimi every possible question, and she's known all the answers.

"Good job," Mr. Lee says. "You'll make an A-plus. Now can you go to sleep?"

"Guess so," Mimi says, her usual smile beginning to creep on her face again. "But I have a hollow feeling right here," she says, pointing to her tummy.

"You think this might help?" Mrs. Lee has come in with a tray on which a cake square and glass of milk sit like on a throne.

Many kids get nervous or overwhelmed when they have to take a test. While Mimi was well prepared for hers and only needed to be calmed down, other students freeze up totally. It can get so bad that the "hollow feeling" becomes a real stomachache that will keep them out of school the next day. Then, of course, the situation gets worse, because the longer a student is out, the more material is missed, which only intensifies fears of future tests.

What's the solution? A teacher with strong skills in the area of *testing,* which these days is often called *assessment.* And in school there are many items, many categories to assess.

16 | Homework and Projects

HOMEWORK IS AN EXTENSION OF CLASSWORK and can be an overnight assignment or a lengthy one spanning several weeks, as in the case of a term paper or major project. When the assignment is creative and not just repetitive, it will

- reinforce a new skill by additional but varied practice,
- extend the lesson by asking the student to do independent research, and
- stimulate the student's curiosity and love of learning.

Definition   Often there simply isn't enough time during class to go beyond the basic introduction of a new skill or subject matter. That's why homework, which is schoolwork to be done at home, and projects, which are research or special assignments, are the perfect vehicles to raise skills and prepare students to show off their newfound knowledge.

Outside-school assignments, whether they are short- or long-range, go a step further. They let students explore some of their own interests, in connection with a given subject, and allow them to develop a better understanding of the topic at hand. In many cases it's during the pursuit of a major science project, or participating in a history fair, or while working on one's own short story collection that students experience the richest learning joy. Through deep immersion in a field of study, they can discover their heart's desires.

Details   Teachers teach beyond school hours with their carefully planned home assignments, be they short or long. First they explain the importance of homework, and then they set standards as to what is acceptable. On the due date, they take up and grade the work done at home.

Kids need frequent and regular feedback on their efforts outside class, so teachers use homework to check on student progress, identify errors, and then make sure the errors are corrected. For that reason homework is checked immediately, so students can benefit from the feedback and teachers can keep track of the progress made. Also, it's important to catch any homework slackers before they develop a serious case of work avoidance.

QUICK TEACHER QUIZ

Now to *your* homework.

Please take time to identify your child's teacher's assessment strengths. The good news is, you don't have to leave home to do this. Just sit down with Mimi after school one day and look over her papers, folders, and notebooks, paying particular attention to her graded homework assignments, reports, and projects. Then read the five quiz questions below and relax, because this is easy. It's all there for you to see and check, if you can answer YES.

YES

____ 61. Are students given homework most days of the week?

____ 62. Is the homework meaningful, related to the lesson, varied, and creative?

____ 63. Is homework always checked, and are expectations clear as to standards for neatness and form?

____ 64. Is there a chance for students to redo incomplete homework and get credit?

_____ 65. Does the teacher let the parent know at once when homework isn't turned in, and is there a set procedure for absentees to make up assignments?

DOES YOUR CHILD'S TEACHER
MAKE THE GRADE?
Here again, three or four YES checks are a good starting point. But if you have trouble coming up with *any* YES answers, or if you're unsure about some of the questions, why not contact your child's teacher? Even better, just ask at the next parent-teacher conference.

Of course, there may be reasons why you can't put a check on some of the blanks. So move on. Instead of focusing on anything negative, notice the signs of excellence in this teacher and then move ahead with discussions and an attitude of understanding and helpfulness. Only in that way will the quiz list be a rung up the ladder to school success.

By the way, while you're thinking about the listed questions, is there anything else about homework that comes to mind? If so, use the blank lines that follow to make a notation of any extra thoughts and ideas you have.

_____
_____
_____
_____
_____
_____
_____
_____

BRAIN GAINERS FOR YOUR CHILD

- Post a homework calendar where Mimi can mark off all her assignments as she does them.

- On days she doesn't have any homework, ask her to read twenty pages from a favorite book.

- Make up a rubric or chart based on the teacher's requirements as to neatness, color of ink used, headings for reports, and so on, and have Mimi check off each item before she shows you her completed homework assignments.

- Help her with "spelling demons," so that carelessly misspelled words won't lower her grades.

- Teach her that cute messaging abbreviations, such as writing *2* instead of *to*, using *&* instead of *and*, and putting little hearts instead of dots on the *i*'s, are unacceptable for schoolwork.

ON A ROLL

- Teach Young to be his own best homework checker.

- Suggest that Young ask Mr. Ennis if he could undertake two Chaucer projects instead of the required one, to offset a low score on his last English project.

- Remind him to ask his teachers for the assignments *in advance* when he knows he's going to have to miss school because of an away game.

- Schedule your kids' medical appointments for teacher in-service days or after school whenever possible.

- When Young gets excited about a homework project,
  help him find extra resources at the university library or
  the appropriate college department in his area.

HONOR ROLL

Once kids treat their out-of-class work as seriously as their in-class work, they're less worried about any assessments, whatever form they might take, and more concerned with becoming better students each day.

That's true for you as well. Soon the whole family will be on course toward being the most supportive and teacher-empowering family in their community. How can that be done? With the same treat Mrs. Lee gave Mimi. Next time you or your husband bake a cake, just take a slice, wrap it in aluminum foil, and ask the school secretary to put it in your child's teacher's mailbox. Tape a note on top that says, *With you as a teacher, keeping my child motivated in school is a piece of cake!*

17 | Quizzes and Tests

AS IMPORTANT AS IT IS to monitor the students' daily progress and achievement by assigning them different types of homework and grading them, it's equally important to keep up with how much new knowledge and skills they're actually retaining during each week and for longer periods. Teaching, therefore, also means assessing frequently how much work has been understood, to what degree it has been absorbed, and how well all the important new skills have been mastered. That can only be done by scholastic checkups. Those are most frequently done by giving quizzes and tests.

Definition Quizzes are shorter versions of tests and cover less material, but both are examinations to determine knowledge. Students can have pop quizzes—unannounced ones—or scheduled quizzes. There are also oral quizzes, when the teacher calls out a set of questions that the students answer, and self quizzes, when a teacher asks students to come up with, for example, ten questions covering the material. Then the kids either answer the questions themselves or pass them on to a classmate to be answered. Some quizzes have ten or twenty questions; others may have only one or two. But no matter what types of quizzes are used, they're part of most lesson plans every day, every few days, or once a week.

In contrast, tests are much longer, at times consisting of 250 questions, or true-false statements, or multiple-choice items, or several essay requirements. Therefore, tests can cover two or three weeks' worth of material or a whole unit. For that reason a test carries more weight in the grading system and counts as much as three, four, or five quizzes, especially when it comes at the end of an important segment. At that point, a big test isn't only the conclusion of a major topic studied but also the foundation for the next one.

Details   Whatever the teacher's particular plan is, all types of assessments are important. While they're sometimes a headache for students, they can be a full-blown migraine for teachers.

Doesn't it sound easy? On Fridays just give a test! But in reality quizzes and tests are far from easy. They require tremendous skill to design, schedule, administer, grade, and record. For that reason, teachers are up late many nights.

Don't the teacher editions of the textbooks include quizzes and tests? Sure, but most teachers go beyond basic printed assessments. Their students aren't textbook cases, so teachers adapt what the text offers to their own classes. Using their own creativity and testing skills, they combine some text questions, rewrite others, and add what's been left out.

However, preparing a quiz or test and giving it is minor compared to the major task of getting kids ready, which means:

- review with them,
- inspire them to study hard, and
- motivate them to give their best performance.

Then comes another tough job: grading all those quizzes and tests. It would be tempting to let some of these materials accumulate because so often teachers have to take them home. There just isn't enough time during the day for the grading. What's extra tough about that is not only the actual grading, which these days can be done by machine, but also recording the scores. That too can nowadays be done with the help of a spreadsheet and grade book software programs used by many teachers.

And yet even this techno test management takes lots of time. Plus, the most creative assessment styles don't lend themselves to machine grading, and even then the teacher needs time to add individual comments.

After all, assessing a student's progress is of little value unless strategies and hints for improvements can be incorporated into the process. A student's mastery of skills doesn't increase merely by having scored 91 out of 100 points and knowing it. It's the suggesting, teaching, guiding, and empowering of the student to get the missing 9 points on the next test that's most important!

That's where the genius of teachers comes in: not in telling their students: "OK, you passed," but in leading them daily to greater heights. For that reason, each quiz and test can never be an end product of learning, but only a start to the next lesson and to the learning leap ahead.

It's often best to have students take part in the scorekeeping, so they can take control in charting their own progress. For that reason also, copies of all their tests need to be on file in the room.

QUICK TEACHER QUIZ

Let's do a quick little checkup ourselves and see how you come out, all right? Not to worry. The YES checklist is only intended for you to find out how to quickly assess your child's teacher's strength in the area of testing.

And that's easy. All you have to do is sit down this weekend and ask your daughter to show you her test folder or that notebook with the deep pockets into which she tucks her quizzes. Look at a few of her tests and discuss them. Then feel relief wash over you. Aren't you glad you're through with school? Finally, just check any question you can answer YES.

YES

___   66. Are quizzes and tests given frequently and are grad-
           ing policies clear?

___   67. Are quizzes and tests graded and returned quickly?

___   68. Are review sheets provided before the tests?

___   69. Are students encouraged to chart their own
           progress?

___   70. Are there written comments on the returned tests
           besides the score, and are folders of each child's tests
           kept in the classroom for parents to look over?

DOES YOUR CHILD'S TEACHER
MAKE THE
GRADE ?

As in previous segments of the Quick Teacher Quiz, three or four YES answers are a good starting point. But if you had trouble coming up with *any* YES answers, or if you're unsure about some of the questions, why not get in touch with your child's teacher? It might be even better to ask your child's teacher about them at the next parent-teacher conference. There may be a reason why your child is tested infrequently or only gets 88 on a quiz, for example, without a written comment. But whatever the reason, please get involved. Ask about the teacher's assessment schedule, focus on signs of excellence, and then do what you can to help the teacher become even better, if that's possible. Under your leadership, a meaningful discussion will ensue. In that way, the quiz list can turn into a vehicle for school success.

And while you're thinking about those questions, ask yourself: Have I more thoughts about testing? If so, use the blank lines that follow to write down any other ideas you have, before they slip your mind.

_____

_____

_____

_____

_____

_____

BRAIN GAINERS
FOR YOUR CHILD

- Two days before Mimi has a test, ask her to write down what she thinks will be on it, and then go over the answers with her.

- Give her a quick quiz every morning as you drive her to school or wait with her for the bus to pick her up.

- E-mail her three review questions from work, so when she gets home she has an e-quiz from you waiting for her. You got mail from Mom!

- Make sure she keeps a folder holding all her quizzes, tests, and review sheets.

- Once a month scan her old tests, pick a question here and there, and see what she can recall.

ON A ROLL

- With Young, let him take some timed practice tests. The local bookstore will have examples.

- Ask him to chart his grades and progress on the computer.

- On a day when you feel courageous, ask Young to give *you* a test. Both of you will break out laughing when you realize how much you have forgotten over the years.

- Ask Young to ask his teachers what their retesting and regrading policy is.

- Be sure to celebrate Young's and Mimi's scholastic successes. That way you'll encourage them to keep striving for a better grade-point average.

HONOR ROLL

That kind of positive forging ahead is infectious. In no time you will want to make the honor roll, too. That means you'll distinguish yourself as the most supportive and teacher-empowering parent in your community. One way to do that is by showing your appreciation for all the many things teachers do. Design a simple CERTIFICATE OF EXCELLENCE with your word processor, print it out, fill in the teacher's name, and frame it. One ordinary school day, when your child's teacher is out of the room, have the maintenance staff set it on her desk.

What a simple and meaningful planned act of appreciation!

18 | Positive Grading and Feedback

OK, THE BIG TEST IS OVER. Now it's time for the finer points of checking on the results. How does a teacher use grading and feedback as a springboard for better and more learning?

Well, how would your physician use your yearly checkup to get you to eliminate any health-risking habits? Maybe charting various observations—such as your weight, blood pressure, and cholesterol level—would lead to discussing them, or perhaps to a warning not to overeat or veg out again. That would be that.

But for a teacher that's just the starting point. Of course, when handing back the quizzes or graded homework or projects, a teacher may make a general comment such as, "If you're disappointed with your scores, I suggest you study longer next time or put in more effort."

Definition But then the teacher's real work begins since teachers thrive on the increased performance of their students. Teaching isn't complete until all members of the class push forward to reach their potential. That certainly calls for savvy grading (evaluating or giving a grade) and feedback (giving information about the results of a test).

How do teachers do that? They give frequent and regular messages back to the students but with a positive twist. That entails sending the parent a progress report as often as possible, but at least at the halfway mark of a grading period, so that improvements can still be made. That's why, even though they may have student helpers to check homework or simple assignments, teachers must personally monitor the progress of all kids, ask them to go over what they missed previously, and check the corrections, and then the teacher can congratulate the kids on their improvements.

Other times teachers may ask students to check their own work by displaying the correct answers with the help of an overhead projector. That's a good time for the teacher to comment on the degree of difficulty of each item and to praise everyone in class who got that item right, while pointing out what the key point might have been, and noting that even those kids who missed it this time will surely get it right next time.

In this way, the teacher's discussion doesn't dwell on mistakes but opens doors to increased mastery. The teacher will never let a student fail without providing a menu of options as to how to make up failing work and learn from it.

Overall, the grading and feedback strengths of teachers rest on a knowledge of child behavior. All kids want to do well in school and at least make a B-. Few children are happy with C's, or average grades, and even fewer like grades below a C. And no child ever wants to flunk.

Details   For that reason, teachers will never put kids into a position where they're guaranteed to fail or score low. That will result in only two things: a dislike of the subject matter, teacher, and school or a strong urge to cheat—neither of which is good. So teachers give kids plenty of review time and supervise the test-taking so carefully that no student can cheat. Then they grade *positively.* They give full or partial credit whenever possible. And instead of making student papers drip with red ink, they write encouraging comments in the margins and a *Much improved!* or *Way to go!* at the end of the paper or on top.

While they do so, they have high expectations and expect good students to get better, the better students to become the best, and the best students in class to have an immediate chance to tackle the material of the next grade level.

There's no glass ceiling for school kids, only a wide-open firmament and a sturdy ladder up provided by parents and teachers. For that reason, teachers need a plan for all kids not making at least a B–. They should be allowed to

- retake the test,
- redo the homework assignment,
- do the project better or do another one,
- complete extra-credit work, or
- prove in some other way that the lesson has been learned.

This goes for kids caught cheating as well. They must be given another chance because a student cheating is only asking the teacher, "Please, help me learn." That way, the child presents the teacher with what is so heartwarming—a chance to take a student from nonlearning to true understanding of a subject. Guide a student to success!

QUICK TEACHER QUIZ

Wow! What power teachers have. Makes you want to change your career and enroll in education classes, doesn't it? You don't have to. Just to appreciate what teachers do routinely is a great step. Another is for you to take a breath and find out how your child's teacher rates in the positive grading and feedback strength. There's nothing to assessing this. Just sit down with Mimi, look at her most recent test grades, and ask her a question or two. Then record what you find out. If you can answer YES, check the blank.

YES

____ 71. Is the students' work graded fairly, and does the teacher allow no cheating?

____ 72. Are halfway grading period averages (interim reports) given, so improvements can be made before report cards come out?

____ 73. Is there a way for students to retake tests, hand in missing work late, make up assignments, and do extra-credit work?

____ 74. Does the teacher have high expectations and high standards?

____ 75. Are detailed comments provided on the interim reports and report cards, in addition to grades?

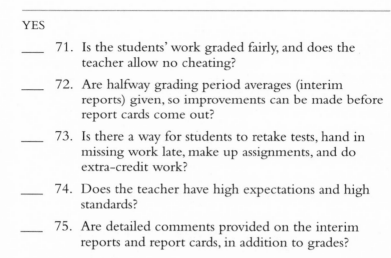

DOES YOUR CHILD'S TEACHER **MAKE THE GRADE?**

While there are exceptions, three or four YES checks are a good starting point, if they include number 71. But should you have difficulty coming up with *any* YES answers, or if you're unsure about some of the questions, why not contact your child's teacher? Better yet, ask your child's teacher about them at the next parent-teacher conference. There may be reasons why you can't put a check on some of the blanks. Rather than focus on negatives, look for positives—the signs of excellence in this teacher. Then start a meaningful discussion. In that way, the quiz can serve as a road map for more school success.

While you're pondering the questions, can you think of more about grading? If so, use the blank lines that follow to make a note of any other thoughts and ideas you have, before you forget:

_____

_____

_____

_____

_____

_____

BRAIN GAINERS FOR YOUR CHILD

- Spend one evening with Mimi, explain the different test types to her, and praise her for paying attention.
- Send a copy of her best spelling tests to Grandma or a favorite aunt.
- Keep a school success folder for each of your children.
- Let Mimi decide what quizzes and tests she wants to save.
- Take all the positive comments Mimi's teacher makes on various assignments, type them on one sheet, and post the sheet prominently at your house.

ON A ROLL

- Help Young memorize a basic essay exam outline and put it to use.
- Tell him to move his desk as far away from other students as possible, so they can't copy his work.
- Make sure he takes an active part in his school's academic honor society.
- Find out of he can sit in or audit a class on a test day in a nearby college.

- Network with other parents to get a tutorial center established in your neighborhood and have Young help out. By helping other students to strive for excellence, Young will continue to do his best.

HONOR ROLL

Once on the honor roll, you will want to stay there. You want to keep on being the most supportive teacher-empowering parent in your community. How can you do that? Just ask your child's teacher. Send a note or an e-mail as a thank-you for doing a great job, then add, "Is there anything I can help you with this semester?"

19 | Exams and Standardized Tests

"HELP! I'M DROWNING!" That's the cry of many teachers these days when they take the time to realize that they're up to their necks in tests. In addition to those they control—weekly quizzes and unit tests and exams at the end of the grading period or semester—they now have to give many tests they have no control over. It's actually not that they mind. They know how important intelligence and diagnostic tests are, and they acknowledge the importance of the PSATs and the SATs. What's really adding to their workload and stress is the recent new emphasis on standardized tests. Those are examinations administered by the state with very precise instructions for timing and scoring.

Definition   This is true in all the public schools in the United States. Since President George W. Bush's new initiative—the No Child Left Behind Act—was enacted in January 2002, every state has begun to stress standardized tests more than ever. During the phase-in period, each state must institute an annual testing program in reading and math for students in grades three through eight and have it in place by 2005–2006. Two years later, more tests for other subjects and other grades will be on the national agenda.

All these tests are formal written examinations of knowledge, designed to put pressure on schools to improve their student performance. In fact, the new law gives states the power to take over any school system where students do not measure up.

The aim, of course, is school accountability. For the past twenty years, one school reform after another has taken place on the state level; by setting national standards it is hoped all our schools will be urged and uplifted toward true excellence.

Details   That's why teachers now have an ever-increasing testing schedule, which overall is welcome. The national affirmation of the importance of scholastics gives teachers the chance to upgrade their curriculum and raise their academic expectations. Teachers and students *want* to be held accountable.

Giving annual assessments motivates class members to work harder. And for teachers it's a great opportunity to see how well their best teaching efforts pay off. They can use the most creative review and reteaching methods, identify early on those students who need more help, and work with parents to extend the classroom to the dens and kitchens of the country, as they send home study hints, handouts, and heaps of helpful how-tos.

Then the whole community can make sure that no child is left behind.

After all, the goal of major examinations and statewide tests is to measure the strengths of each student and to pinpoint the weaknesses, so they can be quickly overcome. That's what goes on in our classrooms anyway each and every day. That's why we have such gifted men and women involved in teaching.

QUICK TEACHER QUIZ

What have you learned in this chapter? Can you now assess any teacher in the country as to how he or she measures up in this particular strength? More important, can you find out where your child's teacher stands? To do so, you don't have to go far, only to your den or child's room and have a talk with your son or daughter. And then at the next PTA or parent-teacher meeting chat with a few moms and dads to get their opinions. Then use the same simple system you've used so far. Just check the *yes* answers. Are you ready?

YES

___ 76. Is your son or daughter well prepared for major exams and standardized tests?

___ 77. Does the teacher work with or tutor students who need help?

___ 78. Does the teacher suggest additional materials and resources for parents of kids needing more help?

___ 79. Does the teacher give plenty of practice tests before exams and state-mandated tests?

___ 80. Does the teacher offer extra materials for kids who are above grade level and thus open even more doors for them?

DOES YOUR CHILD'S TEACHER
MAKE THE
GRADE ?

As before, three or four checks are great, especially if they include number 76, but of course there are always exceptions. If it's hard for you to come up with *any* YES answers, or if you're unsure about some of the questions, why not discuss your concerns with your child's teacher? There may be many good reasons why you can't check off every item. So, rather than worry about that, be glad of the signs of excellence you discover. Begin a dialogue. In that manner, the YES-to-success list will be a vehicle for increased school success.

While you're thinking about those questions, can you come up with more about the subject of increased testing? If so, write down any thoughts and ideas you have on the blank lines that follow, before you forget. Then take this book with you to the next teacher–parent conference.

_____

_____

_____

_____

_____

_____

BRAIN GAINERS
FOR YOUR CHILD

- Know all about the required state exams and find out what kinds of questions are on them.
- Have several practice sessions with Mimi.
- Make those practice sessions fun by interspersing them with laughs and lollipops or some other small treats.
- Teach Mimi to relax before and during tests by taking a deep breath and telling herself that testing isn't such a big deal.
- Tell Mimi that guessing is better than leaving blanks.

ON A ROLL

- Teach Young not to get hung up on one particular problem but to skip it and go back later.
- Sit down with Young and once a week work through an SAT practice booklet with him.

- Check with the librarian at Young's school for recommended books on testing strategies, plus websites and super software programs.

- Enroll Young in a school-sponsored or private or commercial test prep class, and have him start or join a test-study buddy group.

- Be cheerful and positive as you encourage Young to do well on his major exams and empower him to continue his quest to be the best student he can be.

HONOR ROLL

That will spur you on to aim for the honor roll, too. Yes, you really want to be the most supportive and teacher-empowering parent in your community.

How can you do that?

Look over the answers you got when you asked your child's teacher about what you could help with this semester. Then carry out whatever the teacher mentioned. Network with a few other parents and plan an impromptu cookout, except this is going to be a cook-*in* in the teachers' lounge. After first getting the go-ahead from the principal, have all your friends bring in their indoor grills and serve homemade soup (concocted the night before) and the most delectable grilled ham-and-cheese sandwiches. Mm-mm, yes. Delicious!

20 | Time to Evaluate

IT'S TIME AGAIN TO MEET THE REAL DEAL—three teachers who stand out. And while they're again introduced to you under the headings of good teacher, better teacher, and best teacher, you know it is *your* vote that counts. You will have to make the final decision as to how you assess these fine educators. Let's meet them.

GOOD TEACHER

Levi Bernstein, blond and of medium height, is newly married, and he and his wife are expecting their first baby. That makes every teaching hour extra exciting for him because, as he surveys his tenth-grade classes, he wonders which one of his bright students his own child will be like. And what a great chance his career is to prepare himself for that day. The students in his classes are therefore doubly important to him.

Levi comes from a family of professors. His father teaches in the medical school and his mother in the school of nursing—both at the state university. Levi always knew he too would become a professor some day, but then he found this job, which suits him to a T. He can try out his various theories of what makes children learn best, and hopefully by the time little Levi—they already know it's going to be a boy—is in school, he'll have it right. In effect, his classroom is Levi's lab.

It helps that he has five classes with similar students, so he's keeping notes on what changes he makes during the day while especially concentrating on the outcomes—the results. Levi's goal is to find a surefire method of getting each student in each class to perform at a skill level of 95 percent or above. Nothing less will do.

So Levi's tests are brilliant. They vary from class to class and are definitely unpredictable. One time he has nothing but true-false statements, another time only multiple choice, the next time a combination, and so on.

He's slick, too. While his first period gets a test with 25 questions, his second period gets 25 *different* questions. Third period gets 5 questions from the first quiz and 5 from the second quiz, all randomly selected, and another entirely new set of questions added on, and so forth. There's never a chance to cheat on Mr. Bernstein's tests by quizzing students from his earlier classes. That would teach you more stuff, but it wouldn't help you pass. You'd still have to know the chapters that are covered inside out on your own. Bummer!

But even as the students complain, they're glad. They know all the hard work pays off. Mr. Bernstein's classes always score extremely high on final exams and statewide tests. Kids may sigh and groan now, but they sing and grin later. "Mom, Dad, I'm in the ninety-third percentile of my grade level, whatever that means."

Mr. Bernstein knows what it means and thinks, "Darn! Back to work. Next year my students will do better than that."

BETTER TEACHER Taken from a report written by a student:
Nobody at Willside Middle School can outwalk Mr. Uttley, you know. Reminds you of that speedy little dude in that ancient TV show that was always swinging his arms and strutting along a mile a minute. Mr. Uttley, he's that fast. And he talks that fast and is everywhere. Maybe there are two of him, you think?

Whenever students sit down after lunch and work "together" on their homework, he's there and says, "Remember, no copying!" When students pass a textbook to each other as one class leaves and another comes in the room, he pops his head in and says, "No sharing textbooks!"

Whenever a student is in the library hurriedly printing out a report, Mr. Uttley jumps out of the stacks and warns, "Hey, better rewrite that and in your own words, or I'll charge you with plagiarism." Then he takes out something that looks like he's going to give you a speeding ticket. Man-oh-man.

See, in addition to teaching, Mr. Uttley is also the assistant principal. Part-time. That makes it tough to be his student. You can't get away with nothing. I mean *anything*. That also makes it wonderful, because the man is smart. Keeps up with every student and knows you from the moment you walk in his class. That's because he taught your whole family already and knows what to expect. Your older sister Wanda is responsible for that. Why'd she have to be so smart?

Anyway, Mr. Uttley is the person most talked about. And how he makes you work. The moment you step in his room you know exactly what to do. You never waste time. And he's always trying to get you to study harder. Recently he's been talking to Mr. Bernstein, maybe that's the reason.

Worst of all, Mr. Uttley follows you home! Of course, not really. How could he with all the students in school? But this is what he does. You get a quiz back, or your notebook that he grades every weekend. Why doesn't he take a break sometime and go fishing?

But no! He has to spend every Saturday afternoon checking everybody's work. Or like you get the posters and reports back that you and your group presented last week, and you quickly take a peek at your grade—it's a B+, good enough. Then you forget about it until that evening when you get out that quiz or your notebook and look it over, whatever. You know your homework: Correct all the mistakes you made and explain why you made them (in a paragraph with complete sentences, and this class isn't even English)! And there is Mr. Uttley in your face!

No, I told you already. Not really. But on the back of that quiz, or whatever you just got back, there's a whole story written by him in his handwriting with lots of extra questions. Just when you thought today's homework was easy because all you missed was two items. Now you've got to work for another hour. And what's worse, maybe you're making another mistake. Then that man will pile on more "correcting" homework the next day.

And then you can't help it. Dang. You glance at the back of that poster you got back. What a relief; no lengthy comments there. But what's this? There's a textbook page number written in ink. Man, you want to pretend you didn't notice it, but you know what'll happen. At the beginning of class tomorrow, Mr. Uttley will, like, call on you. "Tell the class what you found out last night that will give all of us a clue as to what today's lesson will cover!"

Of course you don't want to look dumb. So you read that page, twice!

But other than making you work hard, Mr. Uttley is an all-right guy. Walks too fast, like I said. If only he'd slow down he wouldn't have so much time left for his long comments. But it's amazing how those comments poke you in the ribs, more than any number or letter grades. You wake up at night and think about them and him. And really, you get determined to show him next time and make 100 on that science test. Bet I can do it too before the year's out. Just wait.

BEST TEACHER Walking with a bounce although she is fifty-four, Anna Liu seems to have an over-supply of energy. She is 5 feet 5 inches and a smidge rotund. Her straight black hair swings as she walks, her smile is contagious and frequent, and she speaks with the hint of an accent. She comes to school at 7 A.M. every day, although the official teacher starting time is 8:30, and she never leaves before 6 P.M. although she could go home at 4. And when she goes home, she's always loaded down with a briefcase and more schoolwork under her arm.

The reason she has so much take-home work is that she's meticulous. She has files upon files, all containing cross-referenced work sheets and study suggestions for whatever skills her students don't have at the beginning of fourth grade but will by the end of the year.

Plus, she has a folder—prepared the week before school started—in which she keeps the predicted academic gains her kids should make, based on available data, such as IQ and test scores from previous years. But she always doubles the prediction and makes a pact with herself that her students will gain two or three years in math.

That means she has a tough road ahead, but she's not alone. She has enlisted all the parents; instead of assigning homework only to her students, she always includes work for the parents too. And each day she not only grades her students, she makes comments on the tests, quizzes, and projects addressed to the parents. On report card day she issues personal notes to every parent because she thinks of them as her home teaching assistants.

Another thing she does is always put two grades on each student's quiz or product, the one the student could have made and the actual one.

So she dangles a carrot in front of each child, then reteaches her lesson at lunch or after school. She also allows every student (who wants to) to retake quizzes. Furthermore, she sends home a perfect paper with each graded work sheet or test so parents and students can study at home and work on the child's weak spots.

Once a month on Saturday morning she asks the parents to come to her room, so she can point out what material will be next in the lesson plan and what assessments she'll use. If a parent can't come, Anna makes it a point to visit them at home. If a parent works the late shift, she makes an appointment and talks to them during their supper break at the plant.

Parents are in awe of Mrs. Liu's dedication. "It's my way to pay back this great country," Anna says softly, when pressed as to why she seems to devote every minute of the day to her work.

Tears collect in the corners of her eyes whenever she thinks of her childhood home so far away on another continent. How hard life was then. Oh, and all those tragic things that happened to her family. . . .

"Anyway," she says, hurriedly blinking back the wetness, "teaching isn't work. It's fun."

It *is* fun, especially for her students, many of whom barely made C's the year before. Now they are invited to make A's. And when they bring their skills up to that level, Anna introduces them immediately to more advanced work.

Her students remember her as the one teacher who made them feel smart. Even students who come from underprivileged homes suddenly have huge plans.

Anna Liu can change not only students but lives.

YOUR CALL

Now it's time for your decision: Which of the three teachers you just met do you think is the best teacher? If you can't make up your mind, just pretend you're a judge instructed to choose which of the three should receive a special award. Who has your vote for good, better, or best teacher? My answer comes later in the book's final chapter.

TEACHER OF THE YEAR

Visit your local teachers' college or a university with a school of education and find out who heads up the teacher training program. It's often an experienced education professor who is assisted by advanced graduate students or former teachers, who have not only the classroom experience but also the academic training. For the past seven years I've been one of those fortunate teacher trainers, and it has allowed me to work with many of the best new teachers. Now you want to meet some of them and invite them to speak to the teachers in your child's school. Nothing fires up experienced teachers more than a fresh new crop of educators brimming with energy and enthusiasm. You can almost pick out the future Teachers of the Year already.

Ask the school principal for permission to bring in one or two of the best-in-class young teachers and then watch the enthusiasm of those young educators spread.

Part V: Beyond the Lesson

FIFTH | Teacher
STRENGTH | Personality

The function of education is to teach one to think intensively and to think critically.

—MARTIN LUTHER KING, JR.

KIEFER, THIRTEEN, AND KIERAN, FIFTEEN, are another brother-and-sister pair. They're glad their names aren't run-of-the mill. Their household isn't either, but that's something they *don't* like.

You see, their dad, who used to make a huge income, just lost his job with a dot-com company that folded overnight. *Wham!* At first Kieran and Kiefer were glad. They thought it meant he would finally have more time for them. Instead, he hasn't been able to find a good job and now works ten hours a day in a home improvement warehouse that's an hour's drive away. So where before he was at least home physically, though Kiefer and Kieran never dared to disturb him in his home office, now he's totally gone from 7 A.M. until way late at night.

These days he can't ever just come straight home without having to chill out first in some bar, or someplace like that. That's what the kids gather from hearing their mom and dad raise their voices at each other, which they do a lot.

Worse is, most days, Mom is gone just as many hours. Her long schedule is caused by her trying to make up the difference in Dad's income. Now she's got two jobs. She works as a child care worker during the day, plus part time in the evenings as a home health aide. And that stresses her out. So when she does come home, all she usually does is gulp something down and head for her bedroom. She's always tired and not in the mood for small talk, let alone hearing about any problems.

Dad's been sleeping in the guest bedroom recently because he doesn't want to wake up Mom when he gets in. That's his excuse, but the kids aren't dumb. They know there's more to it. They just hope Dad can get a better job soon and things can get back to normal.

Now Kieran, who's just come home from school and immediately moved to the kitchen to pull out something for supper, worries it's already too late. Why? Because of that phone call. Before she went into the kitchen, she checked the answering machine like always. It was blinking up a storm, and she thought maybe that cute boy from Advanced Algebra was calling. But no, it was all about Kiefer.

He's in junior high, skinny as a rail and taller that she is, but such a *baby*. And now he's messed up royally. According to the message on the machine, he has skipped school for the past two days. Fortunately Kieran erased it right away, so her parents won't find out. But how long can she keep it from them?

She knows that midterm exams are coming up for both of them. Since Kiefer missed the last two days, which were review days, he'll probably flunk and then—

Her worried thoughts are cut off by the sound of the back door. Her brother is home. "Come in here, you idiot!" she yells, folding her arms and waiting until the boy sidles in. "Where have you been yesterday and today?"

He can tell she knows. "In the toilets."

"All day long?"

"Yeah. Me and a bunch of other boys just ducked into a different one every time another class started."

"Bet that was fun," she says sarcastically. "I understand the boys' rest rooms are filthy." She starts sniffing. "Do I smell cigarettes?"

Kiefer looks sheepish. "Not on me. I didn't smoke, believe me."

"Yeah, right. You just sat on the commode all day and twiddled your thumbs."

"No, but—"

She holds her hands over her ears. "I don't even want to hear what you did, OK?"

"Are you going to tell?"

"You bet, unless—"

"Oh, no. Oh, no. Dad's going to kill me. And Mom's going to ground me like forever. My life's over."

"—unless you come with me right now. I have this teacher I can talk to. She'll know what to do. Last month, when I got caught cheating?"

"You, Miss Perfect, cheating?"

"It wasn't really cheating, just something I copied." Kieran rushes her words. "Anyway, this teacher helped me make it right. I trust her. And she wrote me the nicest note later. Anyway, she's always talking to kids and getting them out of stuff. Come on, let's go see her. She works in that after-school program. . . ."

This anecdote illustrates a vital role teachers play, apart from the teaching of their lessons. They also serve as role models and counselors for students who find themselves on the verge of getting into serious trouble and desperately need someone to turn to, someone they can trust.

Let's take a close look at the *most important* teacher strength there is, and that is their personality, character, and genuine caring for kids. Much of that comes through to students first via the teacher's communication skills.

21 | Communication Skills

TEACHING IS ALWAYS DONE IN FRONT of an audience. The class may consist of twenty-five kids or five, but it's a performance. And what a performance! Just imagine an actor having the same audience day after day and basically the same script—except for the details—and trying to make that same old stuff come alive over and over. That's some challenge. If you don't believe me, try it sometime.

It would seem that we would cut teachers some slack, but we don't. On the contrary, we look at teachers quite critically. We take in their overall appearance, their subject knowledge, their experience or inexperience, and, most of all, how they come across to us. Just as actors are judged by their voice quality, gestures, and facial expressions, so are teachers examined by the way they communicate—in many more aspects. To start with, few actors have to write their own plays, right?

Definition To communicate means to exchange thoughts and messages by speech, signals, and writing; teachers do this every day through their lesson plans and the comments they make. All actors do is memorize lines someone else wrote; teachers have to come up with Act I (an introduction to their lesson) and develop their material all the way to Act V (the final activity and testing). Actors work on motivation—their own—as they play a certain character; teachers not only have to motivate themselves but also their whole class. Actors don't communicate with their fans in writing (except for signing autographs); teachers, on the other hand, interact constantly, verbally and in written form, with their primary audience—the students—and their secondary audience—the parents.

Details   Teaching requires excellent communication skills, including several specifics. For example, teachers have to have a *presence*. They must assert themselves through calmness, confidence, content knowledge, and caring about their students and their subject. That way they come across to their audience as an authority, and what an impressive one!

Naturally, to rate as an authority, teachers have to excel in the basics of oral and written communication. That includes speaking well and using good grammar. They must have an above-average vocabulary and a love for words. They must be able to write neatly, spell correctly, and express their thoughts in well-written paragraphs. Not for teachers is the chicken scratch favored by many physicians!

Teachers are role models, after all, and kids learn best from daily interaction with a verbally talented teacher. Correctness in speaking and writing rubs off. That's why teachers pride themselves on the way they deliver their explanations, write notes home, add comments to graded book reports, journals, portfolios, and report cards, and write personal notes of encouragement.

What teachers are especially proud of is their talent to present even "boring" information in an exciting way. One skill that helps here is assertive body language. Direct eye contact with the class, both with those students who concentrate hard and those apt not to, is most useful. So are good posture and appropriate gestures, such as pointing out tasks listed on the chalkboard or items posted on the bulletin board. How stimulating it is for students to see their teacher moving energetically around the room and speaking from different vantage points. First dropping to a whisper, to get the kids' attention, and later shouting in praise over the fact that all students have done their homework—those are great tools teachers have!

In addition, teachers these days are computer-skilled and -equipped, which makes sending notes home to parents and students much easier. Several parents can be notified at once that their kids "forgot" their homework, for example, and review sheets can be forwarded to all students whose scores have been sinking. Yet teachers have to set an example and teach students that computer spell-check programs aren't as smart as advertised. Example:

> Spell-check: There big yard lyes a cross town.
>
> Student check (after the teacher points out the errors): Their big yard lies across town.

QUICK TEACHER QUIZ

Now it's time for another check—one you will carry out. Can you tell how your child's teacher measures up in communication skills? To find out, all you do is reread the teacher's last note or e-mail, think back to the last phone call you received, or the last talk you two had, and ask Kieran how she liked the last lecture the teacher gave in class.

Then use what you find as the basis for answering the following five questions. Check only if you can answer YES.

YES

____   81. Does the teacher spell well, write neatly, and use correct grammar?

____   82. Does the teacher communicate a message of praise and encouragement to the students?

_____ 83. Does the teacher speak fluently, using a rich vocabulary?

_____ 84. Does the teacher have excellent oral presentation skills?

_____ 85. Is the teacher computer-skilled?

DOES YOUR CHILD'S TEACHER
MAKE THE GRADE
numbers 81 and 82.

As in the earlier sections of the Quick Teacher Quiz, three or four checks are a good starting point, especially if they include

If you have trouble coming up with *any* YES answers, or if you're unsure about some of the questions, there may be a problem. Yet rather than worry about it, why not concentrate on other signs of excellence? Then start to get to know the teacher better so you can be of help. In that way, the quiz list can be a vehicle for school success.

While you're thinking about these questions, can you think of others on the topic of communication? If so, use the blank lines that follow to write them down before you forget:

_____

_____

_____

_____

_____

_____

_____

BRAIN GAINERS
FOR YOUR CHILD

- Have Kiefer find errors in spelling and grammar in a newspaper, then discuss with him what the correct word(s) should be.

- Ask him to scrutinize street signs and restaurant menus from now on and tell you when he finds more mistakes.

- Every so often make a grammatical mistake on purpose, so he can catch you.

- Teach him to read out loud with expression and emotion.

- Write him a special note of encouragement once a week and tuck it under his pillow.

ON A ROLL

- Tell Kieran that the content of any essay is more important than the mechanics, but that her grade can suffer if it's not proofread.

- Give her a book of positive poems, life-affirming and joyful ones, and help her memorize a few.

- Ask her to write a cheery note to a classmate who seems to be down.

- Give her confidence in speaking to a group by practicing with her over and over before she does it.

- Teach her how to construct computer-generated charts and maps to make her oral presentations more impressive.

HONOR ROLL

The better your children's communication skills become, the
better their grades will be. And as they now shoot for the honor
roll, you want to do the same thing. In your case that means
being the most supportive teacher-empowering parent around.
How can you do that? By showing off *your* good communication skills. So write a letter to the editor of your newspaper in
which you sing the praises of your child's teacher. Well done.

22 | Attitude and Respect

SOMEONE SAID THAT NO TASKS IN LIFE ARE HARD if you have a good attitude. True, I'm sure, but for teachers it's never a matter of *if*. They *always* need to have a good attitude, each and every day, just to keep going, because they do the work of a dozen people. They prepare, research, organize, teach, explain, discipline, motivate, inspire, counsel, test, grade, and empower. They give their students the tools to tackle the whole world.

For that reason teachers need an extra-positive attitude toward any problem that can crop up. For a teacher, every student has unlimited talents; every problem child is a potential powerhouse. And it's the teacher's life's work to tap into that power. That's done by focusing on the endless possibilities and by honing one's "hopeful" skill. In that task, teachers are very fortunate: They get a brand-new crop of kids every year and, like farmers in spring, can start each school year expecting the best season ever. Then, by coupling that good attitude with respect for the new crop of students, teachers can count on great rewards in the year ahead.

Definition A *good attitude* is a positive state of mind toward life, and *respect* refers to a willingness to show consideration and be polite. Both need to be evident in teachers. Teachers must be upbeat and treat everyone they come in contact with with kid gloves. It is better to be over pleasant and respectful than not enough.

Kids respond ten times better when they sense that geniality and respect. If kids notice constant grouchiness and feel dissed, they can't learn. Teachers know that and treat both students and their parents in a polite manner. Even if it's hard sometimes—*especially* then—teachers are courteous, admit when they make a mistake, and try to overlook the faults of both students and their parents.

Details   An active learning community is a lively chain in which every segment is valued and every link is lifted. Parents respond beautifully to the respect given them by the teacher, which communicates itself by the way the teacher invites parents to be partners in their children's school success. What a good feeling it is for parents to be handed the teacher's e-mail address and phone numbers at work and at home (for emergencies), so they can be in touch anytime.

It is even more important for the teacher to take every opportunity to invite parents to call or correspond. For the more that parents are asked for input, suggestions for the curriculum, and ideas for solving a problem, the better and stronger the partnership becomes. As always, the beneficiaries are the students and, in a larger sense, the country and the world. The smarter our kids are, the quicker they can solve the world's biggest problems.

So the teacher who invites parents to be powerful partners and learns promptly via e-mail what's on their minds gets a great insight into the skills and needs of the students. It's like a cyberspace home visit, except the teacher doesn't have to leave the house.

That way the teacher, the parents, and the students all enter the circle not of wanna-bes, but of will-bes. *I will be the best.* That's the instant message pulsing along the strong and vibrant connection.

QUICK TEACHER QUIZ

Let's check out how well that connection is working with your child's teacher. Does he or she make the grade on this strong point? What's so great about examining this particular teacher stength is that you can do it wherever you are—at work, stuck in traffic, or waiting in the checkout line at the grocery store. Just take a few seconds, think about the kind of interactions and contacts you have had with your child's teacher recently, and if you can answer YES, check the blank.

YES

____ 86. Does the teacher respect students and parents?

____ 87. Does the teacher apologize after making a mistake?

____ 88. Does the teacher welcome parents, consult with them, and inform them and appreciate parent volunteer efforts?

____ 89. Does the parent have the teacher's phone number(s) and e-mail address and feel free to make contact at any time?

____ 90. Does the teacher return calls and respond quickly to notes and e-mail?

DOES YOUR CHILD'S TEACHER **MAKE THE GRADE ?** Here again, three or four checks are a good starting point, especially if they include numbers 86 and 88. But if you can't come up with any YES answers, or if you're unsure about some of the questions, why not call or e-mail your child's teacher? Better yet, ask your child's teacher about them at the next parent-teacher conference. There may be reasons why you can't put a check on some blanks. So, rather than focus on anything negative, zoom in on the signs of excellence in this teacher, then be the one to start a meaningful discussion. In that way, the list becomes what it's supposed to be—a vehicle for school success.

And if, while you're thinking about these questions, you think of more about teacher attitudes, don't forget to list whatever comes to mind.

_____

_____

_____

_____

_____

BRAIN GAINERS FOR YOUR CHILD

- Respect Kiefer and his opinion.
- Whenever possible, say positive things about your child's teacher and school.
- Stay in frequent contact with his teachers.
- Before you communicate with the teacher, plan what you're going to say.
- Apologize to Kiefer when you've made a mistake.

ON A ROLL

- Write a note of apology to Kieran's teacher when you make a mistake.
- Don't repeat gossip about a teacher and don't allow your kids to do this.

- Offer your suggestions and your resources for a special unit.

- Volunteer at school, in the office, library, or cafeteria.

- Never interrupt a lesson unless it's a real emergency.

HONOR ROLL

If you show how much you value learning, your children will value it also. That will encourage them to study hard and aim for the honor roll. You, not wanting to lag behind, want to make the honor roll as well. That means, you will want to be the most supportive and teacher-empowering parent possible. So get going, e-mail a few other dedicated parents, and start a new tradition: Once a month on a Wednesday, there will be a free breakfast for teachers, parents, and students in the school cafeteria.

Who pays for it? Maybe the PTA or another parent group. Or perhaps the principal, whom you first ask for permission, can name a source.

If the breakfasts don't work out, why not have a Power Parent and Progress Pizza Party?

23 | Interaction with Co-workers and Community and Carrying Out Duties

TEACHERS! In their hands and hearts lie our tomorrows and all the days thereafter. Fortunately, however, they are not alone in their awesome task of educating our children and, by doing so, improving our future. If teachers had no one to lean on, most of them would burn out within a month. But they have a network of assistants—in the classroom next door, in the lounge and the office at school, and these days even on the Internet. With the click of a mouse, they can message with colleagues in Connecticut, California, Canada, and Cambridge, England. The many challenges teachers face every day are lightened by discussing them with fellow colleagues, following their advice, and getting a fresh look at what's going on.

Few professions have such a close-knit fellowship as school-teachers. They all belong to the one group of which it's said that when they die and appear before their Maker, whoever is in charge at the gates to paradise will push all other newcomers aside and swiftly give the teachers access. "After all, as a teacher you've already been in hell," is supposedly the comment up there, "so step right ahead of everyone else." You may not be inclined to chuckle at this, but teachers always do, even though they may have heard this joke before. They crave a little humor to alleviate their stress, and by banding together with their peers and laughing they feel better.

Teachers get even more benefits from working with other teachers. They can learn the latest teaching techniques, shortcuts to positive results in the classrooms, what's coming down the pike in top teacher trends, and new state and national requirements. Naturally, they join the PTA and other parent-involvement groups. How else can they so directly bond with moms and dads?

Definition   This desire of teachers for interaction—the back and forth mental or physical movement among themselves—expresses itself in their joining various professional organizations. Whenever the opportunity arises, teachers attend local, state, and national conferences. No need to carry the teaching burdens of the world all by themselves when they can access all sorts of answers and actions meant for their benefit.

Details   Teachers today live richer and more connected professional lives and can better understand their colleagues. As a result, they contribute to society not just by the work they do in the classroom and by fulfilling their extracurricular duties at school, but also by giving back to their corner of the earth in every way they can.

As we said earlier, we learn by doing. That's especially true for teachers. Teachers learn to be better teachers by reaching out to their cohorts, their co-workers, their colleagues, and their community. That way, they strengthen their own skills while they develop a deep appreciation for others.

QUICK TEACHER QUIZ

Let's see how your child's teacher measures up in this department. It may take a little time, so try to stop by the teachers' lounge, talk to a PTA officer, or watch the teachers' table at lunch. Also, if you just ask the teacher a few questions the next time you have a conference anyway, you'd learn a lot. But no matter how you go about it, please try to find out the answers to the following questions. Then get out your pen or pencil and if you can answer YES, check the blank.

YES

___ 91. Does the teacher belong to the PTA and/or local, state, and national teacher organizations?

___ 92. Is the teacher active in school committees and education clubs?

___ 93. Does the teacher mingle with other teachers during the school day and eat with colleagues at lunch?

___ 94. Does the teacher attend professional conferences and meetings?

___ 95. Does the teacher speak highly of school colleagues and administrators?

DOES YOUR CHILD'S TEACHER MAKE THE GRADE?

By now you know that three or four checks are a good starting point. But if you have trouble coming up with *any* YES answers, or if you're unsure about some of the questions, carefully and tactfully ask your child's teacher about them via e-mail or at the next parent-teacher conference. There may be reasons why your child's teacher isn't involved in any professional organizations. If so, find out and concentrate on other signs of excellence. Start an ongoing discussion. Then the quiz list will surely lead to more school success, which is its real purpose.

As you're thinking about these questions, can you think of more about teacher interactions? If so, write down whatever else pops into your mind. Do it now before you forget.

_____

_____

_____

_____

_____

BRAIN GAINERS FOR YOUR CHILD

- Join the PTA and other parent organizations and take your child along to the meetings.
- Keep up with their goals and help with their fund-raisers.
- Attend their parenting workshops and suggest, and organize, some of your own about making your kids smarter.
- Volunteer to be parent representative wherever needed and serve as a band booster.
- Help update the student dress code and the student handbook from year to year.

ON A ROLL

- Volunteer to be on any textbook selection advisory committee for the school or school system.
- Work on a beautification project for the school grounds or make a small financial contribution.

- Take Kiefer and Kieran along on any volunteering effort. From age two on, kids want to do good.

- Volunteer to substitute for Kieran's teacher during conferences, if that's possible.

- Call up a retirement home, ask if there are any retired teachers, take them out to lunch at Kieran's school cafeteria, and have Kieran talk to them and learn from them.

HONOR ROLL

Of course, many of these suggestions demand time. If you have none to spare, postpone such activities until you do. In the meantime, encourage your kids to aim high. That will inspire you to follow suit. Extra time or not, you want to make the honor roll too, and that means being the most supportive and teacher-empowering parent you can be.

How? One day at work during lunch, call the school superintendent's office and lodge not a complaint but a heartfelt commendation. Say: "I'm calling to thank you so much for hiring such great teachers, and specifically I'm calling about . . . ." Then go into detail about all the strengths that impress you in your child's teacher.

24 | Professional Growth, Appearance, and Character

WITH EACH FRESH CROP OF KIDS walking through the class-room doors, teachers get an injection of new life from the best generation yet to appear on the face of the earth. Yes, each new class brings with itself the most advanced wave of humanity. Teaching thus involves getting a jolt of adrenaline every fall. As a teacher, you are constantly renewing yourself, just like nature. Does any other profession offer that? If so, I don't know about it. That's why it is crucial for teachers to be at their best too.

Definition   Indeed, the professional growth, appearance, and character of teachers rule. That means their constant developing, their public look, and their moral strength and integrity matter. They matter a lot. For that reason, deep down, teachers love their chosen path. Yes, they grumble, gripe, grimace, and groan. But for most of them it's "Once a teacher, always a teacher." Even those people who stop teaching after just a few years never look at life the same way. They're forever altered. You can't grow every year, even if it's just for five years, and then not stand head and shoulders above your age group.

Details   Teachers are special. They never age, at least not inside. Naturally I'm generalizing. But just talk to the retired teacher down the street. The likelihood is that this man still has a twinkle in his eye even though he is ninety. It has to do with inner growth and with the power a teacher has to create human masterpieces out of that fidgety skinny little boy who was too scared to read in front of the class first time he came to your room and that shy scabby little girl who jumped every time you clapped your hands and borrowed paper clips and tape from you to hold her ragged dress together.

And what did you do, besides practice at lunch with the little boy until he had enough confidence to volunteer for the longest part in the play and besides giving the guidance counselor a small check with instructions to please call the girl in and buy her a new outfit? (And voilà! The girl came in the following week beaming over her brand-new top and matching slacks.) Not much, really. You didn't do any more for them than you did for so many others.

Fast-forward fifteen years. You're walking through the mall when a successful-looking young businessman shouts your name and hugs you so hard your ribs almost crack. Then he introduces you to his wife, a fine-looking girl, and two children, hands you his business card, and says: "This is the teacher who made me what I am today." Then he hops into his shining expensive car and zooms off with his family, while his kids wave at you and throw kisses.

And at that moment you hear a squeal and look to see where it came from. Can it be from that lovely young professional woman who's dropped everything—her attaché case, cell phone, and shopping bags from an expensive store—to fling her arms around you and squeal some more? "Thank you, thank you," she sobs. Her makeup runs but she doesn't care. "I'm just in town to visit my aging parents," she explains. "I work for the UN now, at their Paris location." (Or for a bank in Switzerland or a new global company in Sydney, Australia.) And her aura of accomplishment and capability makes you so proud because you recognize her as that poor little abused girl with all the scabs.

At that very moment every miserable second you ever had teaching is wiped away. Because here you see what your life produced: not just these two stellar young people but so many like them, so many golden stars that you got the chance to help fashion, form, and send forward. And in your mind's eye you can see them all over the country, all over the globe, not just a thousand points of light but tens of thousands of peaks of life that you gave rise to.

The students you taught are now touching so many other lives. In that manner, you were the helper of the Creator. You were the polisher of the human product, the adorner, adviser, advancer. It's suddenly all worth it. Your life wasn't in vain. Stop and think for a moment: How many people can truly say that?

I know you're just dying to ask, Did you ever go back to the village school in Diessen am Ammersee in Germany and thank that Catholic nun who made such a difference in your life? *Yes!* More about that in the Epilogue.

Because the stakes are so high in teaching—we're talking about lives that can make a complete turnaround—teachers have to be professional and neat in appearance. After all, part of their job is "selling" education, so they must display by their appearance and manner what great things education does for a person. And yet they don't need to be stodgy or severe. A sense of humor always helps, especially on a Monday morning when the week ahead might be daunting for kids who have had a rough weekend listening to their parents fight.

Besides that, teachers—in order to awaken a lifelong love of learning—must exhibit that love themselves by taking new classes and working toward advanced degrees. What a special bond it is for a group of students to come moaning to the teacher—"Oh, that biology exam tomorrow's going to be a killer"—and the teacher can smile and say, "I know how you feel. I'm taking an oral examination next week, so I can go for my doctorate."

"What's that?" the students will ask.

Right then and there in that teachable moment the teacher can sow the seeds to several future degree candidates in physics, pharmacy, engineering, and chemistry. And in years to come, new inventions, new treatments, and new solutions to mankind's worst problems will be made, discovered, and found—all because of one shining moment in ninth grade.

Besides looking the part, teachers need to act the part. They want to be worthy of the respect of the students and their parents. Sadly, not every child has parents who set a good example. Someone of good character needs to step in and fill that role. It helps a teacher to be a member of a faith-based group, volunteering for worthy causes, and associating with other selfless people. Wow, what a lesson that is—to see your teacher serve in a soup kitchen, chaperone a community youth group, or join one of the many school-based civic-related clubs and activities.

Classroom lessons might be forgotten in the years to come, but that fund-raising project the honor society undertook with the leadership of the teacher will reap benefits years later. And what *always* remains with any student is the *one* time when they were desperate, when they made a big mistake, and yet in their darkest moment there was a ray of hope. It came from a teacher they had who was willing to listen, to show a way out, and to go the extra mile—just like Kieran's teacher did, when she called Kiefer's school, explained what was going on with his parents, and got the boy to attend an after-school program for two weeks and make up his work. That helpful and caring attitude spurred him on to study hard and pass his exams with flying colors.

QUICK TEACHER QUIZ

Now you're ready for the last Quick Teacher Quiz. Before you take it, give yourself an A+ because you've studied the field of teaching and now understand better what teachers do, what makes them tick, and how you can empower them to do even better. So let's focus on your child's teacher one more time.

Before you read over the following questions, know that this is the *most important* teacher strength of all. It's the one dealing not only with what's inside the head, but also what's in the heart. So look at the questions and answer the easy ones first, such as number 96. Then, through thought and discussion, complete the rest. Afterward go out to eat with some friends or take your child on the weekend.

Congratulations, you did it. You're all done with the teacher quiz, as soon as you read the last six questions. Just check the blanks where you can answer YES.

YES

____ 96. Does the teacher look neat and professional and have a sense of humor?

____ 97. Is the teacher of good character?

____ 98. Is the teacher taking continuing education classes or working on an advanced degree?

____ 99. Is the teacher a member of a church, synagogue, temple, or other faith-based or community groups, a volunteer or contributor to worthy causes?

____ 100. Does the teacher attend after-school events, sponsor or help with school clubs, and are the school's student government, yearbook, newspaper, class councils, and honor society active?

____ 101. Most important, is the teacher willing to go the extra mile?

DOES YOUR CHILD'S TEACHER
MAKE THE GRADE ?

While exceptions exist, know that a check next to question numbers 97 and 101 are very important. Of course, so are the other items, so fill in what you can, by concentrating on the signs of excellence in your child's teacher. And if, while you're thinking about these questions, you can think of more about professional growth, please write them down before you forget.

_____

_____

_____

_____

BRAIN GAINERS
FOR YOUR CHILD

- Make sure Kiefer looks neat and clean every day.
- Work on developing good character traits in him, so he has good values and can make good judgments.
- When he makes a mistake, help him correct it.
- Be sure to let him take part in religious observances in the faith of your choice.
- When you give him his allowance, ask him to use one part for helping others, one part for his college fund, and one part for things for himself.

ON A ROLL

- Always act in such a way that your children can be proud of you.

- Attend school events that take place after school and help co-sponsor or coach a school club or sport.
- Encourage Kieran to join one or two school clubs and athletic teams.
- Help with chaperoning field trips, or getting guest lecturers.
- Most important: Teach both Kiefer and Kieran to be grateful and pray every day.

HONOR ROLL

My last suggestion as to how you can be on the honor roll yourself—be the most supportive teacher-empowering parent in your community—costs absolutely nothing, can be done at home, and is the most helpful one of all. Just send to school every day the best-parented, best-prepared, and best possible student—your child!

Now you know what makes an A+ teacher. And yet that's just the beginning. To know is great, but what to do with your knowing is greater, and not to rest until your knowing bears fruit is the greatest thing of all. That makes you a winner.

Thank you for being that winner!

25 | Time to Evaluate

NOW PLEASE ALLOW ME TO INTRODUCE YOU to the last group of outstanding teachers. As in earlier chapters, you will find them under the headings of a good teacher, a better teacher, and the best teacher. But don't accept my labels. By now you know so much about teachers, you should rank them on your own.

GOOD TEACHER Blond and blue-eyed, Lauren Casey is a seventh-grade math teacher and cheerleading adviser at the largest junior high school in the capital of her state. What a beehive her school is! It has grown rapidly and now has many classes that exceed in size the state maximums. Lauren herself has one class of thirty-nine students and another of forty-seven. There aren't even enough desks in her room for all the kids, so she has to borrow chairs from the cafeteria in case every student shows up.

That's almost every day. She has the best attendance record in the school, and no wonder; Lauren is so engaging and inviting.

But she's really not that pretty. When her face is in repose, it's evident that her eyes are set too far apart and her eyebrows aren't symmetrical, with one being a little higher than the other. Also her nose is too small while her mouth is too wide, and yet has almost no upper lip. But those flaws make her even more beloved by her students because Lauren is so lively and interesting. Plus, she cares little about her looks, wears simple skirts and tops that date back to her high school days, and drives a beat-up gray twelve-year-old Audi that regularly gives up the ghost and has to be jump-started.

And yet Lauren the teacher is a miracle worker who's always surging ahead. That's because she makes her students feel special. From the moment they enter the room the first day, she knows all about them, having studied their records beforehand. And while she expects a lot, she makes school fun by having a birthday surprise for each of her kids, by redecorating her room every month, and by using innovation and technology in her teaching.

She's so creative she invents review games and content puzzles that she e-mails to her students' home computers, so they never really leave Ms. Casey's classroom. Their home is just an extension of school.

Those students not having their own computer can either work on the computers in the school library or come in during lunch and use one of the many work stations in Ms. Casey's room. Or they can borrow one of the many snazzy laptops she's gotten various big corporations to donate. Some of those corporations also pay for Internet access and other costs for her less privileged students.

So Lauren's room resembles the future of education, but with a twist. Instead of just coolly managing the technology aspect and keeping her students busy nonstop, she's a human dynamo that propels all kids to do their best.

Students often find personal messages waiting for them on their screens at home or even on their phone answering machines or pagers. Lauren has even invented her own cute messaging lingo. For example, ST4T means *Study for the test*. And XPCT100 means *I expect a grade of 100 from you*, and Y-U-CN! means, *Yes, you can* (so don't give up)!

But all that's just a part of Lauren's teaching. The essence is her human connection with her students. She expects each of them to outdo her in the future, which won't be easy since she's constantly keeping up with the best teaching practices, is enrolled in the doctoral program at her university, and sometimes even takes a group of her underachievers to her evening college classes with her—after getting their parents' permission—just so they can see how exciting it is to be on a college campus.

While a lot of teachers complain when they're assigned to sponsor the cheerleading team, Lauren welcomes it. "With my schedule I don't have time for working out, but the afternoon practice sessions force me to," she explains. "I don't ever want my squad to be ashamed of me, so I exercise with them." That makes her team work that much harder, on and off the field.

And just as Lauren's students apply themselves more every week, so does Lauren knock herself out more and more. She's bringing education into the future, and the future to education. Her students work hard and love it. They love learning, because they love Lauren.

BETTER TEACHER In the same sprawling school building, Maria Rosa Lopez, a young art teacher given to wearing Birkenstocks and bright pant suits of the softest materials, buzzes along but on a different wavelength. To her, art isn't only collective works of beauty created by mankind but also expressions of kindness and caring by the human heart.

"It's a real two-way street," she says.

Therefore, half her teaching deals with the serious study of the ancient and modern masters from all around the world and with sparking her kids into appreciating and attempting similar artistic pictures or designs in paint or sculpture.

Fact is, Ms, Lopez is so talented herself that she can quickly sketch whatever she wants the kids to do on the chalkboard. Plus she knows the lives of famous artists inside out and can deliver a lively lecture on art history at any moment. Being bilingual, she can do this in two languages and is studying a third.

She also knows the curators and schedules of all the art museums in the state so well that she can schedule her field trips for when the most magnificent traveling exhibits come to town. Plus, every year she takes a group of her advanced art students and their parents on a trip to Madrid, Rome, or Paris.

But that's still only half of her teaching. The other half is what's even more important to Ms. Lopez. "I teach to change the world," she says. So just to get kids to understand art and be able to pull out whatever talent they have—and they all do!—is only step one. Step two is empowering them to use their creations to make life better for others.

So watch out: One week the art classes are devoting their time to painting landscape scenes in acrylics; then they study the art of framing. Next thing you know, every new homeowner through the Habitat for Humanity program gets a chance to select a favorite picture—free.

With the help of Ms. Lopez and their parents, the kids hold an afternoon reception during which the excited homeowners have first pick of the exhibited paintings. The paying public is second, and every bit of cash goes for much-needed postage.

The reason? With Ms. Casey's and her students' help, the budding artists have already scanned photos of their paintings onto the art department's website, so that Habitat for Humanity families or beneficiaries of similar programs overseas can make their selection. Since it's expensive to ship the paintings, Ms. Lopez and her students have more fund-raisers.

One of them involves the new shopping center in town. Sculptures by Ms. Lopez and her students already adorn the center court. But twice a month they have permission to set up a booth where for any contribution—PAY WHAT YOU FEEL LIKE! their cheerful sign says—the students draw portraits of children whose parents request them.

Charcoal sketches are popular, but so are the much more time-consuming likenesses in oil, that the students work on as independent projects at home and later deliver to the parents.

For a break, Maria Rosa introduces her students to the history of greeting cards, and before the major holidays she has them do their own designs, vote on the three best ones, and mass-produce them. Then she splits her classes into two groups, one that wants to personalize the cards for inmates and the other that wants to do the same for forgotten rest-home patients, people staying in hospitals or rehab centers for a long time, and this year—for the first time—for the city's homeless.

Distributing the greeting cards presents another way to be creative. Naturally some can be bulk-mailed, but others have to be handed out in person, notably those going to the homeless population.

That has sparked interest in the home ec classes, which meet in the room across from the art studio. Now the home ec kids are knitting scarves to go with the greeting cards. Winters can be harsh here.

Meanwhile, Ms. Lopez has already planned what new projects to encourage her kids to undertake come spring. And the kids and their parents are already guessing what it might be. "Never a dull moment in *her* class," they say with a sigh, and smile from ear to ear. They look at the art club membership cards Ms. Lopez issues to every participant. They read, VOLUNTEER FOR THE ARTS, with the words FOR and ARTS crossed out and replaced by the words FROM and HEART:

VOLUNTEER FROM THE HEART! Surely, that's Ms. Lopez.

BEST TEACHER Mrs. Zora Epstein has neither the knack for badgering corporations into contributing computers to her program nor the time to whirl from one worthwhile school and community project to another. And yet her students remember her forever. Why? Let me explain.

A middle-aged woman with graying hair which she pins up every morning so securely that only on windy days when she

TIME TO EVALUATE

has outside lunch duty would a tendril dare to escape, Mrs. Epstein dresses in timeless no–nonsense suits in dark colors and wears only a nice pin or ring as an accent piece. That's all. Her shoes are leather but sensible too.

As a matter of fact, everything about Mrs. Epstein is sensible and understated. Should you meet her after work, you'd hardly notice her. She looks like an older businesswoman or an office manager for an old law firm: conservative, steadfast, and reserved.

But just wait until you meet her in the classroom. As a young girl, Zora wanted to go onstage. It didn't work out, but she has gobs of dramatic talent and a magical voice that sounds both melodious and captivating and can play tricks on your ears.

When her students listen to her read from *Death of a Salesman* with their eyes open, they watch their talented teacher's hand movements and hear her great voice pronounce every word beautifully. But when they close their eyes, then they can picture the troubled Loman family right away. Another time, when Mrs. Epstein chooses *The Grapes of Wrath*, students, even boys, can't help but cry when they hear—via the teacher's voice—how terrible the Okies' dust bowl conditions were. John Steinbeck portrayed their pain so realistically it can be felt even today.

Amazingly, Mrs. Epstein often doesn't even use a book. As soon as the bell rings and the kids are seated, she just raises her hands in a let's–get–quiet gesture, and the class falls silent. Then she begins to quote a paragraph or two in her incredible voice, which can express every human emotion.

Early in the school year, she has a unit of poetry planned. She begins by reciting, "Beauty is truth, truth beauty,—that is all ye know on earth, and all ye need to know," from Keats's "Ode on a Grecian Urn."

And from that she segues smoothly into Langston Hughes's poem "Harlem," and by the end of the hour the class is not only visibly moved but also changed. At lunch the constant criticism of principal Bill Bates's desire to play classical music alternating with the rock or rap the kids want is suddenly over. "Beauty is truth," the kids say. "So why don't we, like, you know, give Big Bad Bates a chance?"

"Maybe there is something to his dinosaur music."

Another time, the senior class is having a fund-raiser to collect money for textbooks for a newly constructed school in Afghanistan, and Jay, the meanest freshman in school, jumps on a bench in the lobby and shouts a few lines from "Harlem":

> "What happens to a dream deferred?
> Does it dry up like a raisin in the sun? Huh? . . .
> Or does it explode?"

He goes on at the top of his voice: "Know what I'm saying? I'm saying let's let 'em have some books!" He crams a wrinkled $20 bill into the locked collection box, after which he gets permission from Big Bad Bates to take it around to various classes during homeroom period. The final amount collected is stunning.

What's even more stunning is that Jay isn't even a member of Mrs. Epstein's class. He was just loitering in the hall that day she taught the poem, but he remembered it!

Mrs. Epstein's influence goes far beyond this. A few months later, the committee in charge of choosing the theme and decorations for the junior prom decides to downscale this year. Money not spent on the prom will go toward a scholarship for a senior who can't attend college without it. The scholarship— hope is that Jay will get it eventually—is named the Soar with Zora scholarship, and that's not all. These same juniors also start a national From Prom to Prominence movement that encourages other high schools throughout the country and the world to spend less on big bashes, and use the saved cash for a lasting contribution, as they're doing.

What's Mrs. Epstein's secret to her success? Not the way her room looks, because nothing in it is out of the ordinary, though it's neat and clean and has all the essentials. Yet something there has a far-reaching influence.

What is that something? It's her incredible intellect and talent, which is also recognized by her peers. She's the head of the English department, nationally board-certified, and several times has turned down a state position on Teacher Quality. "I can't give up my universe," she says, meaning her classroom.

Recently she wrote a popular book, *Teacher Success on a Shoestring,* which lists numerous strategies to encourage excellence in students without spending a penny. "We have all the teaching tools already—the masterpieces of the past and the records of genius, whether in literature, science, or history," she writes. "Great achievement is our heritage. Let's tap into it, so every student can access the excellence within."

What Mrs. Epstein has done is exactly that. She has opened her students' eyes to the wonders of the world. Even years later, when her former students meet, they greet each other with a quote they learned in her room. And she goes on, presenting selections of the best works of mankind so far. Through her, writers from across the centuries and the continents speak to her classes.

To Zora, quality teaching means using quality materials that speak for themselves and teach themselves. By following this philosophy, she has touched lives of many thousands and has instilled in her students a love for the subject and for what's greatest within ourselves—our power to make ourselves better and those around us.

For that reason, Mrs. Epstein will never die. Even when she stops teaching, her work will live on and her inspirational quotes will be remembered. Many of her students will pick up her habit and read important books to their kids, if not *in utero,* for sure when they're born, as bedtime story supplements.

Others will post famous quotes on the family bulletin board and inspire their own children to think about what makes the quotes so great. Still others will simply live the best lives possible because they were once taught by Zora Epstein. Teachers can never tell where their influence stops. They touch every corner of the earth, not only now but for eternity.

YOUR CALL

Now it's your decision. Which of the last three do you think is the best teacher? Just for a moment, pretend you're a judge, instructed to determine which of them should receive a special award. Who has your vote for good, better, or best? Here is my answer: It all depends on the student.

You see, just as there are many kinds of quality teachers, so are there all kinds of quality students. And no matter how good they are, both teachers and students change over the years. As teachers advance in their careers, they may emphasize one strength over another. For a few years they may work hard to increase their planning skills. Then they may focus more on their student management skills. At other times during their working years, they may concentrate on their testing skills and results. Or they may make continuous progress in *all* areas.

Often the way teachers grow and develop during their thirty or more years in the profession depends not only on what they first bring to the teacher's desk but on how the school climate molds them, whether they have strong mentors, and if professional excitement abounds. A dynamic principal has a tremendous responsibility here.

Some teachers may go through several years of rapidly acquiring new skills and then level off when teaching conditions become difficult; often all such a teacher can do is just keep doing the job. Other teachers start out slowly, like a tiny flame in the fireplace, and—after gaining confidence or having had one extraordinary student—they catch on in a major way and burn bright for the rest of their careers.

This is where you the parent come in, as the observer and well-meaning mentor. You are the circle starter for the teacher, the one-man or one-woman support system. You light the spark among the faculty.

Meanwhile, the students have their own progressive path. They may start out needing a very kind and compassionate teacher and then move on to becoming independent learners, needing only an instructor to point them in the right direction. Other students, if there is turmoil and disarray at home, may hunger for a quiet and orderly classroom atmosphere and a teacher who goes dependably by the rules. Yet a few years later, the same students may need a teacher who constantly stimulates their thinking by employing the most creative lesson plans.

So which of the fifteen teachers you have met is truly the best? That depends on your child. If Kieran is making good progress and is happy in class most of the time, congratulations! She has the best teacher for her at this particular grade level. But if she's frequently unhappy in class, or scared of the teacher, or makes low grades even though she is studying hard, or if she develops a dislike for school, then her teacher isn't a good match for her.

School is too important to let our kids' complaints slide. Any student who studies conscientiously, does homework, has good attendance, and still isn't pleased with school deserves to be helped. Often it's all about some small misunderstanding. The student feels disliked. Or the teacher feels the student is just coasting, satisfied with a B− that could have been an A.

Luckily you, the parent, will step in and find out what the problem is and then offer all the assistance and support you can to make sure both child and teacher are empowered to excellence.

It's the way a teacher responds to your comments and suggestions that's the *real* measure of their quality. Whether a teacher is good, better, or best is in the eye and ear of the learner. Those three words really are only labels for what the purpose of this book is: Teachers who make the grade. Once we have every teacher making the grade, they're all teachers of the year!

TEACHER OF THE YEAR
Who is the TOY for your state and the TOY for the nation? Find out as soon as you can, then invite that person to come and speak to the teachers at your child's school. Why not have these teachers learn from the best? Sometimes these education stars chosen as teachers of the year are booked way in advance, but most of them take a year off from their regular teaching duties to do just that: speak to schools. So get busy and see what you can do. If you can't get the state's first choice, maybe you can get the runner-up. These caring and tremendous teachers all want to make an extra contribution. Maybe you can obtain tapes featuring these special instructors. At any rate, go directly to the top, the state department of instruction. Ask who's in charge of the state selection process. Contact that office and get going. Winners can only win if they enter the arena. You did and you do, so congratulations! And again, thank you!

Epilogue: What Else, Besides Teachers, Must Make the Grade?

Only in growth, reform, and change, paradoxically enough, is true security found.

—ANNE MORROW LINDBERGH

In addition to teachers, the school as a whole must make the grade too. What makes up an A+ school? To find out, glance at some of the following checklists and, then visit your child's school, look around, and record what you observe. It's simple. Just put a check when you can answer YES.

TOP SCHOOL CHECKLIST

Top schools exist in every state. While they vary from location to location, most of them share the same traits. They all honor student excellence and support what it takes to achieve it.

Now see how your child's school compares to these top schools. All you do is check the blanks for YES.

School Grounds

YES

____ Are the grounds safe, and is there a security or safety officer?

____ Are they well maintained and well lighted?

_____ Are they attractive, and is the U.S. flag flying proudly?

_____ Are announcements posted about upcoming events and achievements, and are there spirit/pride posters?

_____ Is there plenty of parking for parents and visitors?

Buildings

YES

_____ Are buildings safe, well lighted, and spick-and-span?

_____ Are there posted rules about visitors' signing in, no guns, no drugs allowed, and so on?

_____ Is the entrance inviting, the lobby impressive?

_____ Do air-conditioning and heating systems work properly?

_____ Are security measures stated and in place and are there metal detectors, for example?

Halls

YES

_____ Are the halls clean?

_____ Are they safe and well lighted?

_____ Are there identifying signs in the halls, and are room numbers with teachers' names well displayed?

_____ Is student work posted, and are awards displayed in trophy cases, as well as important historical documents (such as the Constitution)?

_____ Are water fountains and trash cans provided?

Rest Rooms

YES

____ Are floors, sinks, and toilets clean?

____ Is there no graffiti?

____ Are they stocked with toilet paper and soap?

____ Are there mirrors and trash cans?

____ Are faculty rest rooms sufficient in number and well supplied?

Library and Media Center

YES

____ Is the library well supplied with books, computers, and a host of audiovisual material?

____ Is there a busy but studious atmosphere?

____ Is a wide range of student projects exhibited, such as paintings, science projects, book reports, and poems?

____ Are new materials added constantly, and is there a list where students and parents can request new books?

____ Are there friendly and helpful librarians assisted by friendly and helpful students?

Cafeteria

YES

____ Is the cafeteria clean, friendly, and inviting?

____ Are student art and products displayed?

____ Are healthy foods served with a variety of choices?

____ Are rules posted for students to clean up after themselves, giving consequences if they don't?

____ Are cafeteria workers friendly and welcoming to visitors?

Gym

YES

____ Is the gym clean, well lighted, and with rules posted and safety precautions in place?

____ Is it busy yet orderly, and is the athletic program thriving?

____ Is it well equipped and well run by an excellent PE staff?

____ Are the schedules of upcoming sports events and past champions and victories posted?

____ Are student-made spirit/pride posters and slogans in place?

Office

YES

____ Is the office clean and inviting, with seating areas, flowers, student work, and pictures of graduates?

____ Is information quickly available, and does the office staff know where each student is at all times?

____ Is the office well-organized, with a polite staff well-trained in making announcements?

____ Are secretaries helpful, and do they have a lost-and found box and mailboxes for teachers?

____ Is someone in the office trained in first aid, and is there a school nurse?

Guidance Department

YES

____ Is the guidance department inviting and attractive?

____ Is the staff helpful and proactive in dealing with the problems kids may have these days?

____ Does the staff have a wealth of materials, from problem-solving to career guidance to college prep information?

____ Are there seating areas and chill-out or "quiet" rooms, and are the counselors knowledgeable about teacher stress and the methods of coping with it?

____ Are the counselors highly trained, and do they go beyond the call of duty?

Teachers' Lounge and Workrooms

YES

____ Are the teachers' workrooms up-to-date with telephones, computers, printers, copy and fax machines, and paper and other supplies?

____ Is the teachers' lounge a large, friendly place with seating space for teachers, plus a sofa on which to stretch out?

____ Is there a refrigerator, microwave, coffeemaker, and cold drink machine?

____ Does the PTA or another organization supply the coffee, tea, cream, and sugar?

____ Are there flowers, samples of teacher artwork, teacher letters, and inspiring teacher poems and memos posted, including schedules, upcoming events, and thank-you notes from parents?

Principal/Assistant Principal

YES

____ Is there a student handbook, detailing all aspects of the school routine, that's updated each year to reflect the changing times?

____ Does the handbook explain school rules, the dress code, the consequences for rule-breaking and the steps to follow in case of complaints, grading disagreements, or bullying, and is discipline well enforced?

____ Does the principal's office have a seating area, and are student achievements and the school motto or vision statement posted?

____ Is the principal among the friendliest staff members, quick to follow up with whatever concerns you and well-liked by the faculty?

____ Are the reading and achievement test scores of the school well above the state average and climbing higher every year?

Superintendent of Schools

YES

____ Is it easy to get an appointment with the school superintendent?

____ Is the atmosphere in the superintendent's office friendly and welcoming, and is he or she respected by the principals?

____ Are student works and achievements from the various schools in the system displayed?

___ Are the school system's vision statements posted, plus the
yearly goals and the academic achievement plan for the
coming year?

___ Is the superintendent a friendly person who responds
quickly to your concerns?

School Board Members

YES

___ Are school board members easy to reach?

___ Are they friendly and knowledgeable?

___ Are they solution-oriented and do they follow through
quickly?

___ Are they open to suggestions?

___ Are you informed as to how you can get on their meeting
agenda, and is that process simple?

PTA (or Other Parent Groups)

YES

___ Are there PTA and other parent organizations and booster
clubs?

___ Are these groups active, with good memberships, and are
students encouraged to be a part of them?

___ Do they bring in keynote speakers on school issues, and is
the public invited?

___ Does the PTA raise funds for the extras teachers need, and
do the members honor outstanding student achievement?

___ Do they have a newsletter, e-mail capabilities, or other
means to inform all parents of the latest educational issues?

Community

YES

____ Is the community supportive, and does it rally around its schools and teachers?

____ Are school fund-raisers well attended?

____ Is there an active school volunteer group?

____ Is a strong mentoring program in place?

____ Are financial rewards and incentives provided by businesses to retain or attract top teachers?

Fast and Final Exam

YES

____ Do the teachers' kids attend the schools in this system?

____ Do the principal's kids attend the local schools?

____ Do the superintendent's and board members' kids attend these schools?

____ Do the kids of the mayor, aldermen, city council, church leaders, sheriff, and other elected officials, leaders, and the professional community in general attend the local schools?

____ Do the former high school grads do well, in college and years later, and do they still fondly and gratefully recall the time they spent in the local schools?

OVERALL SCHOOL OR SYSTEM RESULTS

Here are a few more questions to ask. They're good starting points when comparing schools or school systems.

> What are the achievement scores?

> What are the attendance rates and dropout rates, and how many high school students graduate on time?

> What percentage of students go on to four-year colleges and universities?

> How many students get scholarships to colleges and universities?

> What is the teacher and principal turnover rate?

> How many teachers are teaching out of field?

> How many teachers are nationally certified?

AHA! MOMENT

If the children of the professional educators who work in the school system in which your kids attend school do *not* attend the schools within that system, you have an Aha! moment, a moment when you realize that obviously not everything is as it should be. For if those schools were in tiptop shape, surely *everyone* would send their children there.

So you say, " Aha!" And after that you roll up your sleeves and get busy. For it's no good to see a flaw unless you view it as a chance to do something about it. So draw from all the best practices in teaching and infuse your kids' school with them.

And how do you get hold of those best practices? Easy. First find out where the kids of the leaders of the school system and the community *are* going to school and why. Should it turn out that this is a private school, charter school, or parochial school, you're in luck, because you're going to visit that school, find out what makes that school "better" than the one your kids attend, then "steal" their ideas and implement them at your kids' school. You're going to copy everything that's great. Copying is simple once you know how. And then—voilà!—what a bargain. You will have a first-rate school right in your neighborhood, and you won't have to spend all that tuition money.

Here's what you do, step by step. See the principal or head-master of that other school and ask to visit, for half a day or even just two hours. On that day, get a name tag identifying yourself as a visitor and set out—with this book in hand—so you know what to look for. Then use a red pencil in checking out this school. Does it really deserve more YES checks than the school your kids attend? If so, wonderful. Now you're armed with knowledge. You can report back to your PTA group or your committee or your informal parent pals and start moving ahead. After all, you're a school parent pioneer. You're going to scout out what's missing from your kids' classrooms and teachers. What they lack you will put back!

Assume you come up with a list, short or long. It's even more exhilarating to see how many items on that list can become YES items at your kids' school too.

Because you care deeply, you will be empowered to take your concerns to teacher groups, schools of education and their deans, policy advocates, and other influential leaders. You can also interview graduates of your child's school or school system who are now in college and find out what they believe was lacking back when they went to school—or is lacking now.

Then you can lobby the school board on your local and state level for more money. You can also write lawmakers and request support and funds from organizations and individuals who care. You can also start a website for local school improvement. Call it the winners' circle or Parent-Teacher-Student Partners for

Success. Whatever you decide to do, you will exert a tremendous influence.

Henry Adams said: "A teacher affects eternity." And you—by helping a teacher to become better—empower eternity. What's more important than that?

Personal Note

About my village in Bavaria. Remember wondering if I ever went back years later to visit that pitiful little ruin of a school where a Catholic nun saved me?

Yes, one time I did manage to go back. Because of that nun's influence, I became what I am today, a productive and successful person: teacher, education expert, and author. Just like that skinny little boy and that pitiful little girl whom I taught showed me years later how tremendously my teaching influenced them, I always wanted to thank that kind nun personally.

After I'd been teaching school in rural North Carolina for many years, I finally got my chance. I flew to Munich, went from there to Diessen by car, and found my old home which had escaped a direct hit by Allied bombs during World War II but had been almost uninhabitable when I lived there as a child.

It all came back to me as I took the winding dirt lane from the now-renovated house to the monastery with the pitiful little shack where the nuns had set up school and headed toward the white church and tower that rose above the square. You see, I started first grade in the fall of 1945. Earlier that year, Adolf Hitler had committed suicide in a bunker in Berlin and the Allies had taken possession of scorched-earth Germany. Most of the buildings in my village had suffered damage. Worse, most families had lost a father, son, brother—and those were just the obvious losses.

After six years of war, every German still alive had post-traumatic stress syndrome, except we didn't have a name back then for what we were going through.

We just knew that we ached all over with every breath we took and had horrible nightmares; with nothing to eat, our skinny bellies bloated up from hunger and our bones were weak. For years we suffered from rickets, had lice, running noses, and running sores all over our bodies. Worst of all, we felt constantly ashamed over what had happened to the Jews.

We had no hope and didn't think we deserved to have any. . . .

Years later, here I was walking again to my elementary school, which was now a big building with solid walls, new desks, a clean board, books, maps, and polished floors—a regular thriving little place of learning.

It was summer, so there were no classes going on. When I knocked on the door of the adjoining monastery and asked to speak to Sister Gertrude, I was shown to the director's office, where a heavy-set old lady in a crisp nun's habit received me. I introduced myself, explained where I had come from, and asked to see my former teacher.

"Sorry but she's gone on," the director said.

"That's too bad," I said. I explained how in second grade, Sister Gertrude had changed the life of a sad, skinny little girl, one of eleven hungry kids, made almost mute by war and family tragedy—

"I remember that family," the director cut in. "Yes, they had eleven children. Sister Gertrude often talked about them. She wondered whatever became of them, especially the youngest girl, who could barely function after her mother died. The poor little thing didn't know it and had tried for days to wake up the dead woman—"

"You're looking at her," I said, wiping my eyes.

"I can't believe it," the director said. "You look so—so—"

"Healthy and happy and well off?"

"Exactly."

"It's all because of Sister Gertrude. If she hadn't paid special attention to me, singled me out one time and made me feel proud, who knows what would have happened to me. . ."

The director hugged me. *"Vielen Dank!* Thank you for telling me. We don't often get to see the results of our work."

"No," I said. "I thank *you* and all the other nuns who carry on Sister Gertrude's work. *Vielen, vielen Dank* to you and all the other teachers!"

Later, back out on the square, I felt such joy. That I could have made this journey! That I could have had the chance to come back here! I looked at the flower beds ringing the village square. Weren't the geraniums in bloom such a bright splash of red color against the green leafy background? Didn't the lush roses cluster here and there and nod knowingly in the soft breeze? And didn't that church tower reach all the way into the bright blue Bavarian sky and at this very moment send my words of thanks onward?

Just so, supporting teachers in their teaching sends a message into the future. You can't ever tell how far your influence will reach. Someday maybe your children, your grandchildren, their friends, and their neighbors' children and friends will all be better off because *you* gave a little of yourself to make their teachers A+ teachers.

So, A+ to you! You're a real winner and you make dreams come true. Welcome to the winners' circle!

A great teacher makes hard things easy.
—RALPH WALDO EMERSON

*Better than a thousand days of diligent study is
one day with a great teacher.*
—JAPANESE PROVERB

When you teach. . . , you will reap a hundred harvests.
—KUAN CHUNG

*And when you help teachers teach,
the harvests you reap are infinite in number.*
—ERIKA KARRES

Appendix A: Complete Quick Teacher Quiz

Check the all blanks that apply: Just go check, check, check.
Check YES for Success!

YES

___ 1. Does the teacher provide a handout or calendar of curriculum goals at the beginning of the school year?

___ 2. Does this handout list the statewide and/or standardized testing dates for the year, plus the latest federal education mandates, if applicable?

___ 3. Do you and your child understand this handout?

___ 4. Is parent involvement in curriculum planning and enrichment appreciated and welcome?

___ 5. Are class rolls, seating charts, daily and weekly schedules, emergency lesson plans, and special instructions for special students available for substitutes in a clearly marked "emergency" folder?

___ 6. Is the classroom clean, neat, and arranged logically?

___ 7. Are special rules and procedures posted, along with a map of the school showing which exits to use in case of a fire, tornado, school shooting, or other emergency?

____ 8. Are work stations set up with computers, paper-backs, or reference books, and is there a place to display students' best efforts?

____ 9. Is a daily or weekly schedule posted?

____ 10. Are grading period dates and breaks posted, and are samples of previous student work and previews for upcoming units or otherwise visually stimulating posters displayed?

____ 11. Is the teacher open-minded and welcoming of children with diverse backgrounds?

____ 12. Does the teacher help parents of children with special challenges or with nontraditional backgrounds or arrangements?

____ 13. Is the teacher sensitive to the changes in our society and helpful to all kids whose parents are going through major problems, be they divorce, the death of a family member, substance abuse, or others?

____ 14. Are multicultural posters and artworks displayed that are representative of all ethnic groups, and are there books and materials from a diverse mix of authors?

____ 15. Is the teacher sensitive to all cultures and religions by being inclusive rather than exclusive?

____ 16. Does the lesson plan vary during the week?

____ 17. Is group work included as well as team learning, pair learning, and computer research?

____ 18. Do students have a choice of activities?

____ 19. Are the teacher lectures requiring note-taking no longer than 15 to 30 minutes?

____ 20. Are student-created products and projects, videos, skits, and plays, and written and oral book reports scheduled several times a year?

____ 21. Are books and other materials ready and handouts issued promptly?

____ 22. Do all students get their textbooks, paper, and pencils out quickly?

____ 23. Does the teacher quickly explain what the lesson is about, why and how it will be taught, and what materials will be used, and are key points written on the board?

____ 24. Is attendance taken during the introductory comments and explanations?

____ 25. Does this opening-class process take less than five minutes?

____ 26. Does the teacher get all kids on task quickly, within five minutes after the bell?

____ 27. Is every student's work checked and every student called on at least once during class?

____ 28. Are all students learning something and encouraged to try their best?

____ 29. Does the teacher constantly monitor the class, ensuring a high time-on-task atmosphere for all students?

____ 30. Are there follow-up or extra activities for those who finish quickly?

____ 31. Does the lesson excite all the children and pull them in?

_____ 32. Does the teacher know the subject well and use audiovisuals, including posters, tapes, and other materials, to add oomph to the lesson?

_____ 33. Does the teacher teach briskly, accelerating student progress sometimes yet reteaching other times?

_____ 34. Does the lesson touch on the kids' lives and interests, stimulate their curiosity, widen their horizons, and include various opportunities to respond?

_____ 35. Are the middle and end of the lesson engaging, and does the teacher sum up what has been taught?

_____ 36. Does the teacher include instructional activities that allow students to move around during class?

_____ 37. Does the teacher encourage all kids to participate actively in class by keeping score in a grade book, with a checklist, or on the board, while drawing out the quieter students and holding down the kids who always have their hand up?

_____ 38. Is the teacher able to tell you on a daily basis about your child's work?

_____ 39. Is the teacher's vocabulary appropriate, the grammar correct, and the voice quality good and are the words pronounced correctly?

_____ 40. Are students allowed to work in groups and make presentations, and are they encouraged to use proper English by example and reminders?

_____ 41. Are the classroom rules posted prominently?

_____ 42. Are the consequences posted prominently?

_____ 43. Do the kids follow the rules most of the time?

_____ 44. Are school rules observed outside the classroom?

___ 45. Are the students allowed to suggest and vote on some of the rules themselves?

___ 46. Does the teacher have all students under control and supervision?

___ 47. Are all students, even sleepy or disinterested ones, encouraged, involved, and motivated to participate?

___ 48. Are misbehaving students caught *before* they misbehave?

___ 49. Does the teacher circulate the room constantly and stand by the door during class changes in order to supervise what's going on in the hall?

___ 50. Does the teacher know and use the latest discipline practices?

___ 51. Does the teacher deal quickly and effectively with disruptions?

___ 52. Does the teacher hand out consequences to disruptive students and make sure they comply?

___ 53. Does the teacher keep the rest of the class working quietly while dealing with disruptions?

___ 54. Does the teacher return to teaching smoothly, so the class continues to flow and no time is lost?

___ 55. Does the teacher stay calm at all times, having planned a response for whatever interruptions may occur?

___ 56. Does the teacher praise all the kids in some way every day?

___ 57. Does the teacher help students, especially if they were wrong, by trying to understand why they did what they did, and then expect improvement?

____ 58. Does the teacher give supportive statements about any improvement, be it ever so slight?

____ 59. Does the teacher give feedback to students that encourages them to expand their thinking?

____ 60. Does the teacher validate all kids verbally or with a smile or nod or applause or positive note?

____ 61. Are students given homework most days of the week?

____ 62. Is the homework meaningful, related to the lesson, varied, and creative?

____ 63. Is homework always checked, and are expectations clear as to standards for neatness and form?

____ 64. Is there a chance for students to redo incomplete homework and get credit?

____ 65. Does the teacher let the parent know at once when homework isn't turned in, and is there a set procedure for absentees to make up assignments?

____ 66. Are quizzes and tests given frequently and are grading policies clear?

____ 67. Are quizzes and tests graded and returned quickly?

____ 68. Are review sheets provided before the tests?

____ 69. Are students encouraged to chart their own progress?

____ 70. Are there written comments on the returned tests besides the score, and are folders of each child's tests kept in the classroom for parents to look over?

____ 71. Is the students' work graded fairly, and does the teacher allow no cheating?

___ 72. Are halfway grading period averages (interim reports) given, so improvements can be made before report cards come out?

___ 73. Is there a way for students to retake tests, hand in missing work late, make up assignments, and do extra-credit work?

___ 74. Does the teacher have high expectations and high standards?

___ 75. Are detailed comments provided on the interim reports and report cards, in addition to grades?

___ 76. Is your son or daughter well prepared for major exams and standardized tests?

___ 77. Does the teacher work with or tutor students who need help?

___ 78. Does the teacher suggest additional materials and resources for parents of kids needing more help?

___ 79. Does the teacher give plenty of practice tests before exams and state-mandated tests?

___ 80. Does the teacher offer extra materials for kids who are above grade level and open even more doors for them?

___ 81. Does the teacher spell well, write neatly, and use correct grammar?

___ 82. Does the teacher communicate a message of praise and encouragement to the students?

___ 83. Does the teacher speak fluently, using a rich vocabulary?

___ 84. Does the teacher have excellent oral presentation skills?

____ 85. Is the teacher computer-skilled?

____ 86. Does the teacher respect students and parents?

____ 87. Does the teacher apologize after making a mistake?

____ 88. Does the teacher welcome parents, consult with them, and inform them and appreciate parent volunteer efforts?

____ 89. Does the parent have the teacher's phone number(s) and e-mail address and feel free to make contact at any time?

____ 90. Does the teacher return calls and respond quickly to notes and e-mail?

____ 91. Does the teacher belong to the PTA and/or local, state, and national teacher organizations?

____ 92. Is the teacher active in school committees and education clubs?

____ 93. Does the teacher mingle with other teachers during the school day and eat with colleagues at lunch?

____ 94. Does the teacher attend professional conferences and meetings?

____ 95. Does the teacher speak highly of school colleagues and administrators?

____ 96. Does the teacher look neat and professional and have a sense of humor?

____ 97. Is the teacher of good character?

____ 98. Is the teacher taking continuing education classes or working on an advanced degree?

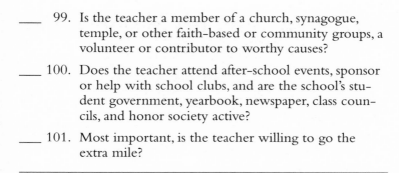

____ 99. Is the teacher a member of a church, synagogue, temple, or other faith-based or community groups, a volunteer or contributor to worthy causes?

____ 100. Does the teacher attend after-school events, sponsor or help with school clubs, and are the school's student government, yearbook, newspaper, class councils, and honor society active?

____ 101. Most important, is the teacher willing to go the extra mile?

Total up your YES answers: 75? 85? 95? No matter how many you end up with, remember this: These questions are basic ones. In no shape and form do they touch on everything your child's teacher does, but they do serve as a beginning blueprint for quality teaching. Please use them as you would any blueprint—*as something to build on.*

Appendix B: Support Systems and Organizations

National PTA

http://www.pta.org
Customer Service Department
330 North Wabash Avenue, Suite 2100
Chicago, IL 60611
Phone: (800) 307-4782
Fax: (312) 670-6783

National PTA is a nonprofit association of parents, educators, students, and others active in their schools and communities.

Learning First Alliance

http://www.learningfirst.org/
1001 Connecticut Avenue NW, Suite 335
Washington, DC 20036
Phone: (202) 296-5220
Fax: (202) 296-3246

The Learning First Alliance is a permanent partnership of twelve educational associations that have come together to improve student learning.

National Coalition for Parent Involvement in Education (NCPIE)

http://www.ncpie.org/
3929 Old Lee Highway, Suite 91-A
Fairfax, VA 22030
Phone: (703) 359-8973
Fax: (703) 359-0972

NCPIE is a coalition of organizations working to create family and school partnerships in American schools.

Appendix C: **Recommended Reading**

Connolly, Theresa, et al. *The Well-Managed Classroom: Promoting Student Success Through Social Skill Instruction.* New York: Boys Town Press, 1995.

Connors, Neila A. *If You Don't Feed the Teachers They Eat the Students: Guide to Success for Administrators and Teachers.* Nashville: Incentive Publications, 2000.

Gagne, Robert M., et al. *Principles of Instructional Design.* New York: Holt, Rinehart & Winston, 1992.

Odden, Allen, and Carolyn Kelley. *Paying Teachers for What They Know and Do: New and Smarter Compensation Strategies to Improve Schools.* Thousand Oaks, Calif.: Corwin Press, 2001.

Palmer, Parker J. *The Courage to Teach: Exploring the Inner Landscape of a Teacher's Life.* New York: Jossey-Bass, 1997.

Price, Hugh B. *Achievement Matters: Getting Your Child the Best Education Possible.* New York: Kensington Publication Corporation, 2002.

Romanish, Bruce. *Empowering Teachers: Restructuring Schools for the 21st Century.* New York: University Press of America, 1991.

Senge, Peter M., et al. *Schools That Learn: A Fifth Discipline Fieldbook for Educators, Parents, and Everyone Who Cares About Education.* New York: Doubleday, 2000.

Thousand, Jacqueline S., et al. *Creativity and Collaborative Learning: A Practical Guide to Empowering Students and Teachers.* New York: Paul H. Brookes Publishing Co., 2001.

Appendix D: Helpful Internet Sites

http://www.4nvkids.com/Providing.htm
   Provide Quality Teaching.

http://www.teachingquality.org/resources/articles/
investinginteaching.htm
   Investing in Teaching, an article found at the website of the
   Southeast Center for Teaching Quality
   (http://www.teachingquality.org/default.htm).

http://www.nctaf.org/
   National Commission on Teaching and America's Future.

http://www.adprima.com/
   A website aimed at education students and new teachers,
   with useful information for all who are interested in
   education.

http://www.projo.com/special/teaching/921c.htm
   Teaching Matters; "Quality of teaching makes the difference."

http://www.pta.org/parentinvolvement/standards/index.asp
   The National Parent–Teacher Association's National
   Standards for Parent/Family Involvement Programs.

http://www.prichardcommittee.org/about.html
   A citizen–advocacy group in Kentucky that has collected
   resources of interest nationwide.

http://www.edu-leadership.com/
> Committed to contributing to the improvement of public education.

http://www.educationnews.org/
> Provides links to major education news articles worldwide and commentary from national education leaders.

http://www.edweek.org/
> Online home of *Education Week*, a publication dealing with aspects of school reform.

http://www.time.com/time/education/
> Online home of *Time* magazine's education articles.

http://www.nea.org/
> Website of the National Education Association.

http://www.ed.gov/index.jsp
> Website of the Department of Education.

Acknowledgments

A special thank-you to Bettina Grahek, outstanding principal and education leader, and to Rebecca Carpenter, for Internet research. Also to June Clark, my agent and guide along the stepstones of my writing career.

At Andrews McMeel Publishing I wish to thank the following extraordinarily talented professionals: Janet Baker and Michelle Daniel, for copyediting; Pete Lippincott, for interior design; Tim Lynch, for art direction on the cover; Chris Schillig and Dorothy O'Brien, editors, mentors, and role models, for their overall encouragement, guidance, and powerful vision; and finally to Erin Friedrich, my A+ editor, for her competence, caring, and character.

224